HONORING
AFRICAN AMERICAN
ELDERS

HONORING AFRICAN AMERICAN ELDERS

A Ministry in the Soul Community

Anne Streaty Wimberly, Editor

Jossey-Bass Publishers
San Francisco

Substantial discounts on bulk quantities of Jossey-Bass books are available to corporations, professional associations, and other organizations. For details and discount information, contact the special sales department at Jossey-Bass Inc., Publishers. (415) 433–1740; Fax (800) 605–2665.

For sales outside the United States, please contact your local Simon & Schuster International Office.

Jossey-Bass Web address: http://www.josseybass.com

Manufactured in the United States of America on Lyons Falls
TCF Turin Book. This paper is acid-free and 100 percent totally chlorine-free.

This book was supported in part by a grant from the Administration on Aging, Department of Health and Human Services. Grantees undertaking projects under government sponsorship are encouraged to express freely their findings and conclusions. Points of view or opinions do not, therefore, necessarily represent official Administration on Aging policy.

Credits are on page 210.

Interior design by Claudia Smelser.

Library of Congress Cataloging-in-Publication Data

Honoring African American elders : a ministry in the soul community /
    Anne Streaty Wimberly, editor. — 1st ed.
        p.   cm. — (The Jossey-Bass religion-in-practice series)
    Includes bibliographical references and index.
    ISBN 0–7879–0351–5 (alk. paper)
    1. Afro-American aged—Religious life. 2. Church work with the
aged—United States. 3. Afro-Americans—Religion. I. Wimberly,
Anne Streaty, date. II. Series.
BR563.N4H66   1997
259'.3'08996073—dc20   96–45781

HB Printing   10 9 8 7 6 5 4 3 2 1   FIRST EDITION

The Jossey-Bass
Religion-in-Practice Series

CONTENTS

PREFACE

The church plays a vital role in the lives of older African American adults. The church is likely the primary, if not the only, voluntary association to which many of these persons belong. Now, as in the past, the church is where many elders receive spiritual, socioemotional, and instrumental support. Indeed, African American churches have had a history of providing important, culturally relevant informal and formal assistance to elders. They have assured the role of elders as both receivers and doers in their communal life when other institutions failed. In this way, churches have served as "soul communities" whose actions have reflected the ethnicultural and biblical injunction to "honor the elders."

We expect the African American church of the present and the future to continue its tradition as a soul community where honoring elders remains an important priority. However, churches are experiencing an unprecedented challenge. They are challenged to minister in ways that adequately address elders as active participants in community life and as receivers of care. They are challenged as well to keep eyes open for emerging issues elders face in what may be called turbulent times for African Americans of all ages. If churches do not move forward forthrightly with these ministries, they will fail to honor elders, who constitute the very bedrock on which the present and future of the church and community are built.

The challenge to churches is brought about by a number of critical changes. These changes include increasing numbers of persons aged sixty-five and over, ongoing severe health and socioeconomic problems among elders, continuing barriers faced by elders in the public sphere, escalating caregiving demands on elders and family members, and the presence of generational conflict and separation. There is no doubt that churches—rural and metropolitan—want to do the right thing with and on behalf of elders. But they must rely on informed and skillful leaders for direction.

Yet the leaders themselves often need help to know what to do and how to do it better, particularly in times of profound change and challenge. Moreover, some leaders need help to envision and articulate the benefit of older adult ministries to the vitality of the whole community, given prevailing beliefs that the future is built around the vitality of youth and young adults. The intent of this book is to provide needed help and guidance for leaders.

Direction of the Book

This book proposes a model of older adult ministry drawing on the African American cultural and religious heritage. It includes cultural and religious foundations for the practice of this ministry. Moreover, it explicates specific current and emerging issues confronting elders and their families that ministries should address, and it describes concrete ways for churches to honor elders' roles as receivers and doers in the community.

We have proposed a ministry that proceeds on the basis of two interrelated values. The first value is *honor*. To honor African American elders means to acknowledge the significance of their years and to treat them as persons of worth. We understand honor to be more than just showing respect, through deference and courtesy. It includes deep appreciation, which we demonstrate through interested listening. We are aware of the special gifts and unique qualities of these people. We convey genuine enjoyment of them as persons and take joy in their participation in and contributions to the community, making room for such participation. Honor also means taking them seriously, which we demonstrate by soliciting their opinions and including them in decisions that affect them. It means serving them in times of need, showing love, conveying appreciation for their humanity, and preserving their dignity. And we honor elders out of our love of God and God's love for them. In actual ministry, we translate our understanding of honor as a value into these concrete actions.

The second value is *soul community*. To speak of the soul community is to speak of an African American community that operates from a sense of "peoplehood" and an appreciation of shared history, shared culture, and shared challenges. We understand ourselves to be a hospitable extended family, with a closeness that embraces us in a bond greater than friendship. We take joy in remembering what we share, making room for it as a valued activity. We act out of commitment and compassion in our relationships. In actual ministry, we translate our understanding of soul community as a value into these concrete actions.

To speak of honoring African American elders in the context of the soul community means to voice a commitment to embody the values of honor and soul community in everything we do. We regard elders as important bearers of history and culture, and we value and assure their place in the community as contributors and receivers of care. We are grateful for their presence and facilitate their roles as stewards. And we assure cross-generational relations as the context for this to happen. We see in them the road ahead for the young and regard what happens to them as happening to the whole community. We respond to their felt needs out of our awareness of their situations, believing that they are entitled to caring response and that God calls us as a community to respond.

Our goal is the well-being of the elders, and we consider our community an "opportunity structure" that connects them with the resources necessary for their well-being. We assure our community's compassionate presence with them in times of crisis, illness, and death, believing that we are connected with one another in both our living and our dying.

The book assumes that churches, guided by informed and skillful leaders, can minister with elders and on their behalf, for their sake and that of the whole community. For this reason, we are writing specifically for clergy, coordinators of older adult ministries, church school leaders and teachers, and other laypersons and family members interested in these ministries. Denominational leaders and seminaries may also find the book useful in preparing persons to be knowledgeable leaders in older adult ministries. Social service providers, too, may find in the book information that is helpful in seeking liaisons with churches for the benefit of elders and family members.

Though many authors are focusing on the importance of the church in the lives of older African American adults, no resource details a comprehensive model for ministry focused specifically on these elders in the manner presented in this book. Much of the present literature consists of reports of studies dealing with the role of the church in the lives of elders. Other volumes focus on the broader topic of the black family and include some references to the role of the church and roles and issues of elders in the context of family life.

How This Book Developed

This book is a teaching resource that reflects the contributors' uses of current literature and their knowledge and research on issues pertinent to present and future older adult ministries. It results from the journey of a faculty team at the Interdenominational Theological Center (ITC) in Atlanta, Georgia. The team began the journey as developers of a core curriculum in gerontology for use with seminary students and alumni, participants in continuing education and certificate programs, and church pastors and leaders of older adult ministries.

The efforts of the team came about through the ITC's participation in a project of the Georgia Multidisciplinary Center for Gerontology for Historically Black Colleges and Universities (HBCUs), located at the Morehouse School of Medicine in Atlanta. Funded by an Administration on Aging (AOA) grant, the project sought to improve the quality of life for African American elders, particularly those at risk of losing their independence. Our participation in this effort evolved from our awareness of the important role of churches and the critical need to prepare church leaders to respond effectively to the increasing number of older members in congregations.

Over the period from 1992 to 1995, the faculty team developed and presented gerontology modules, courses, and community seminars focused on biblical foundations for older adult ministry, social and psychological factors underlying this ministry, and approaches to the practice of the ministry.

As team members, we struggled to discern pivotal elements needed to shape a ministry with elders that could also help build a resource base for churches. We explored the scant research on the church's role in the lives of African American elders. We were guided by our own involvement in older adult ministry and what we learned from older adult ministry participants and from our families. We reflected on our own aging and gained insights from thoughts and images that emerged. We learned from our students and seminar participants, some of whom were themselves older adults. This book reflects our struggling with the imperative to honor our elders and our learning of ways to respond to it.

Overview of the Contents

The contributions to this volume, commissioned expressly for it, detail specific steps in reenvisioning a process of honoring African American elders through the church environment called the soul community. The material is divided into two main parts that consider the foundations of older adult ministries and the practice of older adult ministries, respectively. Readers may read the chapters of each part in sequence for an overview or may consult specific chapters for the specialized information they provide.

Part One is devoted to cultural and religious foundations for honor-bestowing ministry. It contains four chapters. Chapter One, "What Honoring Elders Means: A Call to Reenvision the Church and the Soul Community," written by the book's editor, Anne Streaty Wimberly, describes the important challenge facing African American churches to reenvision ministries focused on elders and based on the values of honor and soul community. Chapter Two, "Tapping Our Roots: African and Biblical Teachings About Elders," written by Temba L. J. Mafico, discloses key aspects of the African cultural and Judeo-Christian heritage of African Americans. Chapter Three, "The Church as a Soul Community," by Anne Streaty Wimberly, explores the nature of the soul community. It includes biblical origins of soul, qualities of relationships, and particular habits that express what it means to be a community that honors African American elders. Chapter Four, "Creating an Honor-Bestowing Elder Ministry," also written by Anne Streaty Wimberly, proposes a ministry model that centers on elders. The model focuses on the goal of well-being of elders, specific directions ministry in the soul community should take, and specific activities the community should initiate.

Part Two is devoted to the practice of ministry in the soul community. In Chapter Five, "Showing Honor Throughout the Life Cycle," Edward P. Wimberly explores the dynamics of relationships with older adults at each stage of the life cycle. Older adults are recognized in this chapter as recipients of care, repositories of wisdom, and resourceful participants in family life. In Chapter Six, "Supporting Cross-Generational Relationships," Edward Wimberly proposes a process for groups to look at their families cross-generationally. The chapter describes African American support system values and the connection between behavioral science theory and cross-generational honoring. In Chapter Seven, "Creating Elder Ministries for Different Locations," Stephen C. Rasor describes distinguishing characteristics of rural and urban elders, particularly the unique problems and needs experienced in each context. The chapter explores what it means for the church as a soul community to honor elders in each context. It describes specific actions needed to respond to the elders as recipients of care and the church's role in implementing these actions in honoring ways. In Chapter Eight, "Building a Helping Network," Anne Streaty Wimberly describes a constellation of connections that churches can make with helpers in the public domain to provide assistance, support, and guidance to elders and family helpers. The chapter proposes a three-phase process for forming an honor-bestowing helping network. In Chapter Nine, "Pastoral Care and Nurture in the Soul Community," Edward Wimberly examines African Americans as worthy recipients of care, and pastoral care as an indigenous initiative focused on the care of souls and as an important response to older adults. In Chapter Ten, "Health, Illness, and Death in the Context of the Soul Community," Anne Wimberly explores the meaning of showing honor in matters of health, illness, and death. The chapter presents ways of promoting physical health, responses churches can give in times of serious illness, and an approach to decision making in life-and-death situations. The final chapter, "Honoring and Sharing Our Elders' Wisdom," written by Edith Dalton Thomas, Anne Wimberly, and Edward Wimberly, affirms the significance of the participation of elders and their role as a resource in the soul community. It highlights their essential contribution to the vitality of the community as storytellers, Bible interpreters, and guides in practical wisdom and ritual life.

Acknowledgments

I am deeply indebted to all of the contributors to this volume. From the beginning of the gerontology core curriculum project through the preparation of this book, they have been a lively, supportive, and committed group. They willingly undertook the process of writing their contributions, accepting critiques, and undertaking revisions. Their efforts have made it possible to include a variety of perspectives, disciplines, and theoretical orientations. For this reason, the contents do not necessarily represent a consensus. They do represent, however, a common desire to contribute to the knowledge and efforts of all persons who are involved in ministries with older adults.

In addition to the gratitude due the contributors, I extend additional special thanks to several more individuals: Mary Williams, whose invitation to the ITC to participate in the initiatives of the Georgia Multidisciplinary Center for Gerontology for Historically Black Colleges and Universities at the Morehouse College School of Medicine set in motion the process that has culminated in this book; James H. Costen, president of the ITC, and Calvin Morris, ITC vice president for academic affairs, who gave unwavering support to the project and preparation of the book; and Edith Thomas, John

Diamond, Ndugu T'Ofori-Atta, and the late Thomas J. Pugh, whose leadership in promoting gerontology in seminary education at the ITC actually predated the core curriculum project.

I wish to express particular and loving gratitude to my husband, Edward, for the special assistance and extraordinary patience he has freely given.

Atlanta, Georgia   ANNE STREATY WIMBERLY
November 1996

In honor of Ndugu T'Ofori-Atta,
elder, colleague, and extended family member

THE EDITOR

Anne Streaty Wimberly is associate professor of Christian education and church music and coordinator of the Gerontology in Seminary Education Initiative at the Interdenominational Theological Center (ITC) in Atlanta, Georgia. She received her B.S. degree (1957) in music education at the Ohio State University, Columbus, and her M.M. degree (1965) from Boston University. She received both a graduate certificate in gerontology (1979) and a Ph.D. degree (1981) in educational leadership with a cognate in gerontology from Georgia State University, Atlanta, and a master of theological studies degree (1993) from Garrett-Evangelical Theological Seminary, Evanston, Illinois. She was a postdoctoral scholar in residence (1981) at the Institute for Religion and Wholeness, now called the Clinebell Institute, at the School of Theology at Claremont, California.

Wimberly's professional background has included public school and higher education teaching in the area of music and seminary teaching in Christian education, music, and gerontology. Her primary research and publication activities have also been in these areas. Her books include *Soul Stories: African American Christian Education* (1994) and *The Church Family Sings: Songs, Ideas, and Activities for Use in Church School* (1996).

Wimberly has served as chairperson of the Multicultural Task Force on Older Adult Ministries for the United Methodist Church North Georgia Conference. She has been a member of the governing board of the Forum on Religion, Spirituality, and Aging (FORSA) of the American Society on Aging; the board of directors of Reaching Out to Senior Adults (ROSA) in Atlanta; and the advisory committees of the Multidisciplinary Center for Gerontology for Historically Black Colleges and Universities at the Morehouse School of Medicine and the National Center for Aging, Religion, and Spirituality.

THE CONTRIBUTORS

Temba L. J. Mafico is Old Testament professor at the Interdenominational Theological Center (ITC) in Atlanta, Georgia. He has been an ordained minister of the United Church of Christ since 1964. He pastored five congregations in Harare, the capital of his native Zimbabwe, while completing his B.A. degree (1970) at the University of London, Rhodesia College. He subsequently became the first black chaplain and teacher at Chikore Mission High School. After coming to the United States in 1970, he earned his master of theology degree (1973) at Harvard Divinity School and his M.A. (1977) and Ph.D. (1979) degrees in the Department of Near Eastern Languages and Civilizations, with a major concentration in Old Testament and ancient biblical languages, at the Harvard Graduate School of Arts and Sciences. He has published articles in the *Anchor Bible Dictionary,* the *Journal of Theology for Southern Africa,* and the *Journal of Northwest Semitic Languages.*

Stephen C. Rasor is associate professor of sociology of religion and director of the Doctor of Ministry Program at ITC in Atlanta, as well as a participant in a rural ministry project. He has been an ordained minister in the United Methodist Church since 1971 and has served as pastor and minister with youth in local churches in Georgia. He received his B.A. degree (1970) in philosophy from Millsaps College, Jackson, Mississippi, and his D.M. degree (1973) from the Candler School of Theology at Emory University. He completed his Ph.D. degree (1984) in society and religion at Emory University. Rasor has served on several United Methodist Church North Georgia Conference boards and committees and has been a teaching parish pastor supervisor. He has also led numerous leadership education events in local churches and at the conference level. Rasor's articles have appeared in *Ministry and Mission, Antithesis,* the *Journal of the ITC,* the *Review of Religious Research,* and the *Western Journal of Black Studies.*

Edith Dalton Thomas is adjunct professor of Christian education and retired registrar and director of admissions for ITC in Atlanta. She was previously associate dean for student affairs and acting registrar at the former Clark College, now Clark Atlanta University, and secretary for student records at Atlanta University. She received her B.A. degree (1948) in business administration and secondary education and her M.A. degree (1963) in guidance and counseling from the Atlanta University School of Education. She also obtained both an M.R.E. degree (1977) and a D.M. degree (1987) from the ITC and a graduate certificate in gerontology (1989) from Georgia State University, Atlanta. She has been a board member of Prison Ministry with Women; a member of the Georgia Consortium for African American Aging, the advisory committees of Reaching Out to Senior Adults (ROSA), and the Wesley Woods Geriatric Hospital Kendall Project Advisory Committee; and vice president for enabling services of Church Women United, all in Atlanta.

Edward P. Wimberly is Jarena Lee Professor of Pastoral Care and Counseling at ITC, Atlanta, where he also heads the Thomas J. Pugh Pastoral Counseling Center. He has been an ordained minister of the United Methodist Church since 1969 and has served pastorates in Winchendon and Worcester, Massachusetts. In addition to his work at the ITC, he has served on the faculties of the Garrett-Evangelical Theological Seminary in Evanston, Illinois, and Oral Roberts University School of Theology in Tulsa, Oklahoma. He received his B.A. degree (1965) in history from the University of Arizona, Tucson, and both the bachelor of sacred theology (1968) and the master of sacred theology (1971), with a major in the sociology of religion, from the Boston University School of Theology. He completed his Ph.D. degree (1976) at the Boston University Graduate School, Division of Theological Studies, in the areas of pastoral psychology and counseling. Among his many publications on pastoral counseling are *Prayer in Pastoral Counseling* (1990), *African American Pastoral Care* (1991), and *Using Scripture in Pastoral Counseling* (1994).

HONORING
AFRICAN AMERICAN
ELDERS

PART ONE

CULTURAL AND RELIGIOUS FOUNDATIONS FOR HONOR-BESTOWING MINISTRY

WHAT HONORING ELDERS MEANS

A CALL TO REENVISION THE CHURCH
AND THE SOUL COMMUNITY

Anne Streaty Wimberly

REVEREND X PASTORS A CHURCH with a membership comprising a large number of senior adults. He speculates that they make up about 40 percent of the congregation of an estimated 150 on the roll. For a long time, the seniors were the "faithful saints," the ones who attended worship services most often. "The seniors were good about stepping aside so that the younger folk could lead," Rev. X noted. "But their very presence seemed to repel the young. The young folks simply would not get involved. . . . Sure, the seniors are important, and the ministry the church offered them was important to them. The church is supposed to honor them, and I think we did honor them as far as we could. But there's no doubt about it, I think we missed out on something. It just seems to me that when the community is separated like we were, there's something about honor that's not real.

"But there came a point," Rev. X continued, "when some seniors, some young adults, and I agreed that enough is enough. The church just isn't supposed to be this way. So they brainstormed what might be possible. They came up with three steps. For step one, the seniors who were able decided to visit one on one in the

homes of the children, some of whom were their relatives. These seniors formed a 'storytelling circle' at the church and invited the parents to allow the elementary-aged children to attend. It worked! In
step two, the seniors and the young adults decided on a church rally
the last Sunday of every month. They planned to have some seniors
tell Bible stories and explain what the stories meant in their lives.
They also asked some children and youth to sing or rap and to have
a hand in leading devotions. The youngsters also role-played the
Bible stories they heard and told what they learned from what they
heard and did. Step three was to make sure that the parents of the
children were involved. They were basically the ones to bring re-
freshments. Also, this step was to make sure that the seniors and
others who needed help were taken care of."

Reverend X's church came alive because the seniors were there
and wanted younger folks there too. But Rev. X is quick to point
out, "I now know what's possible. What happened in my church really worked. But I know that lots of churches out there are stuck at
the point where young and old don't mix, either because of the differences between them or because young folk are moving away. At
any rate, they've got a lot of seniors and not so many young folk.
And the seniors may not be able to make a difference in every case.
But we have to hope somebody can change things."

<hr>

Ministries designed to honor elders are an unequivocal necessity
now and into the future. The challenge to African American
churches is to assure the presence of these ministries and to maintain
honor as the center of every ministry activity. Making this happen
requires an intentional process and an invitation to churches to take
the time to reenvision these ministries.

As suggested by the opening case, the reenvisioning task is a crucial one. It is crucial not simply for churches like Rev. X's but for
every church. The imperative nature of the task derives from the
deleterious effect of the prevailing climate of individualism on the
historical African American sense of peoplehood. In the past, this
sense of peoplehood, this soul community orientation, made possible African Americans' focus on recognizing and responding to
group members' needs. It included an uncompromising assumption
about honor shown to elders. However, the present and future generations are in peril of losing sight of the moral significance of honoring elders and the meaning of the soul community.

It is important, therefore, that our churches consider the direction of their efforts to honor elders and to reenvision how to create an ongoing vital soul community within which honor can flourish. It is important that our churches look deeply at what is happening in ministries with and on behalf of elders, why they are choosing to do what they do, and what is yet to be done and by whom. It is equally important for churches to bring to sharpened awareness the impact of what is or is not happening not only on the lives of elders but also on the lives of every other generation within the community.

Five assumptions underlie the reenvisioning process. The first assumption is that the value and ways of honoring elders are deeply imbedded characteristics of the cultural and religious history of African Americans and can provide present-day inspiration and guidance. Second, present and future ministries designed to honor elders do not come about without ongoing thoughtful reflection. Third, any ministries designed to honor elders are best developed out of a whole community's journey with the elders and not in isolation from them. Fourth, ministries designed to honor elders are ministries that affirm the veracity and vitality of the soul community. Fifth, the way we minister with and on behalf of present elders teaches the younger generations what is acceptable for ministries in their own later years.

Three key matters serve as parameters for the reenvisioning task. The first pertains to the meaning of *honor* and the historical precedents for it. The second involves the meaning of *soul community* and historical understandings of it. The third has to do with the compelling issues in the reenvisioning task. It is to these matters that we now turn.

The Meaning of Honor

Honoring elders is a deeply embedded value in African American life. Stories and beliefs from the African past and the slavery years depict it. The African American belief system draws on Bible images and ideas that emphasize it. Present-day caregivers of older adults reflect it. However, we are in a critical period that demands renewed attention to its meaning.

Honor means acknowledging the significance of the lives lived by elders and treating them as persons of worth. When we act in concert with this understanding, honoring elders becomes both the underlying motivation for our ministry and the activity that defines the ministry process. Motivation for honoring elders goes beyond a mere understanding of honor: it is a matter of the heart.

The honoring of elders as the underlying motivation for ministry focused on them builds on the traditional ancestral African view that presumes that all persons are valued members of God's family and are therefore deserving of honor. More than this, the motive for honoring elders derives from the ancestral view that the actions of persons who honor elders make tangible the elders' experience of God's love (Mbiti, 1990, p. 38). In short, honor as motivation derives from the moral significance assigned it by the ones who do the honoring. In an important sense, it is seen as part of the vocation, or way of being, of the Christian sojourner.

As an activity that defines the ministry process, honoring elders includes the activity of those who honor as well as the activity of the elders. The activity of those who honor emphasizes their sensitivity to needs of elders for inclusion in matters that pertain to them. It also emphasizes their sensitivity to the dual role of elders as doers and receivers in the life of the community. This counters the notion that elders are simply passive recipients of care. It embraces an understanding of at least three roles of elders in the life of community. These are also historical roles. In supporting and facilitating these roles, community members honor elders. The "three R's" of honoring elders—as *recipients* of care, as *repositories* of wisdom, and as *resourceful participants* in community life—reflect the interrelationship of the elders' roles and the community's support and facilitation of the roles through its caring response.

Honoring Elders as Recipients of Care

When elders encounter struggle and need, we honor them by providing care. Honor takes the form of willingness to spend time with elders and concrete efforts to respond to their needs. This understanding of honor is not new. The practice of supporting and responding respectfully to elders as recipients of care has a long history. This history serves as a helpful framework for looking at current interpretations of honoring elders as recipients of care and what may be reincorporated as a response to present-day circumstances.

During the era of slavery, the slave elders were honored and respected by the extended family network. Indeed, Genovese (1974) states that "careful attention to and respect for the aged carried on a classic African attitude" (p. 522). Honor and respect meant that whenever possible, the extended family took on the responsibility of caring for the elders when they were ill and dying.

Genovese (1974) also emphasizes that "the slaves, including the children, looked to the needs of their old people and treated them with a respect and deference that offset humiliation heaped on them by condescending, not to mention unkind, whites." They did all within their power to allow the elders to end their lives with dignity. If some responded to their parents or grandparents with indifference or hostility, "others in the community would step in to assume responsibility" (p. 522).

During slavery, families were included in the activity of honoring elders as recipients of care. Some older slaves lived with their children (Mellon, 1988). Moreover, elderly slaves were not always exempt from work, even though they lacked health and stamina. In such cases, young slaves helped the elders so that the work quotas were met (Martin and Martin, 1985).

Prior to the end of slavery, freed slaves formed benevolent societies at the community level that were designed to address the particular needs of widows and orphans. Two of these societies were the Free African Society, chartered in 1789 in Philadelphia under the African Methodist Episcopal (A.M.E.) Church, and the Brown Fellowship Society, organized in 1839 in South Carolina (Kaplan, 1973; Martin and Martin, 1985).

Following the end of slavery and well into the twentieth century, the African American community's regard for elders appeared in a variety of forms. New benevolent societies, including burial societies and credit unions, emerged in African American churches as means of providing aid and services to elders and others in need. Homes for elders also became a characteristic charity sponsored, staffed, and supported by African Americans from churches and other benevolent groups. African Americans considered the earliest homes for black elders as means of affirming the worth of elders and of according them respect and care not given by larger society (Martin and Martin, 1985; Du Bois, 1909; Wimberly, 1979).

As the African American institutional church grew, church programming targeted visitation ministries with sick and homebound elders. Churches organized adult church school and Bible study classes specifically oriented toward the needs of adults, including elders, to be spiritually enriched and to seek answers to life issues. Some churches sponsored senior citizens' centers and nutrition sites in response to the needs of elders in the congregation and the community.

The long tradition of honoring elders as recipients of care continues to develop in many African American churches as a primary form of ministry. In this regard, the importance of the process of reenvisioning older adult ministries lies in the opportunity it affords churches to consider what is yet needed in this dimension of honoring elders. The importance of the reenvisioning process also lies in the opportunity it affords churches to determine if honoring elders as recipients of care is balanced with the other honoring activities.

Honoring Elders as Repositories of Wisdom

By honoring elders as repositories of wisdom, we encompass a regard for what elders know by virtue of their years of living. This activity assumes that what they know about African American history and culture can provide a kind of awareness and even rootedness not otherwise possible. It also assumes that there is something about their lives, be it tragic or hopeful, from which the younger generations can learn and use to guide their future sojourn.

Like honoring elders as recipients of care, honoring elders as repositories of wisdom has a long history. Africans and African Americans have historically placed a high value on the wisdom of their elders. Paris (1995) points out that African ancestors held to the belief that "the normative value of tradition is embodied in those who have lived to see old age and are now close to the ancestral world" (p. 144). Africans still believe that owing to the importance of the wisdom and influence of their elders, children must be made to feel strong ties to the generation of their grandparents and even their great-grandparents (p. 144).

During slavery as well, elders were honored by the value placed on them simply for being the eldest. Their status within the extended family was affirmed by references to them as "Aunty," "Uncle," "Mama," or "Papa." The slave community also considered elder slaves as repositories of community wisdom, wisdom that grew out of experience, as well as spiritual wisdom. Older men who learned to read and write not only interpreted the Bible for others but also taught others to read and write using the Bible (Mellon, 1988). Moreover, older men and women were the storytellers who bolstered the spirit of the young and passed on community sayings, beliefs, and values (Bradford, 1971; Mellon, 1988). And it was the elders who "studied" herb medicine and accumulated folk wisdom and used what they learned to tend to the sick (Genovese, 1974).

The community looked on elders as possessing "mother wit" or practical wisdom—what Paris (1995) calls "the excellence of thought that guides good action" (p. 144). It entails a kind of intuitive knowing how to judge a given situation and what, if anything, to do about it.

The kind of honor accorded elders on the African continent and in North America during slavery, because of the value placed on their wisdom, continued after slavery. When African Americans moved to cities during the great post-emancipation migration, grandparents were often left behind. However, many parents sent their children to spend time with grandparents during school holidays in order to allow time for the elders' influence and for inculcating values and their practical importance (Paris, 1995).

Although honoring elders as repositories of wisdom continues today, often in the form of grandparents' roles as primary caregivers for grandchildren (Taylor, 1988; Aschenbrenner, 1973), there is evidence of its waning as a dominant activity. Hilliard (1995) refers to a process of "cultural surrender" whereby time is not taken to know either parents or ancestors (p. 69). Without elders who may serve as positive models, younger generations are increasingly left to rely on substitute "wisdoms" from peers and the media. This situation prevents historical grounding of the young and diminishes the possibilities of their gaining awareness of positive parenting and grandparenting roles.

It is important that any ministry-reenvisioning process take to heart existing disparities between traditional understandings of honoring elders as repositories of wisdom and current understandings. Likewise, it is important to consider the needs of families for guidance in making honor-bestowing generational connections.

Honoring Elders as Resourceful Participants in Community Life

We honor elders by recognizing that their belonging to the church community and actively contributing to its life to the extent they are capable expresses their humanness and enriches the community. Elders should not be expected to withdraw from participation in the community by virtue of their advancing years. To do so is tantamount to disconnecting them from the central context of religious meaning and the vitality of human interactions. Mbiti (1990) describes the African ancestral understanding of this necessity: "To be human is to belong to the whole community, and to do so involves participating in the beliefs, ceremonies, rituals and festivals of that community. A person cannot detach himself from the religion of the group, for to do so is to be severed from his roots, his foundation, his context of security, his kinship and the entire group of those who make him aware of his own existence" (p. 2).

During slavery, elders functioned as communal heads who taught the young how to pray and instilled values in them (Martin and Martin, 1985; Mellon, 1988). A diary entry of missionaries in slave communities also tells of three hundred catechized black children kept under the watchful care of an elderly black female (Crum, 1951).

In the aftermath of slavery, older African Americans played significant roles in the growing African American institutional church. In the present, as in the past, the church serves as a focal point not simply as a network of support for elders but also one for the exchange of material goods, services, and emotional aid (Chatters, 1988). Indeed, in numerous instances African American church activities are geared toward the interests, support, and participation of older members. Moreover, these members exhibit significant control of religious instruments and ritual in African American churches. Older men number greatly on deacons' and trustee boards, and older women are represented in large numbers on mothers' boards and in women's auxiliaries.

In the present, as in the past, the elders are the members most likely to be called on to pray and to be church historians. They also sing in choirs, serve as ushers and communion stewards, engage in visitation ministries, and lead church school and ministries with young people. In these ways, elders continue to be honored as resourceful contributors to community life. These opportunities make it possible for elders to feel important and do something important (Jackson, 1971; Lewis, 1971; Mays and Nicholson, 1969; Dancy, 1977; Wimberly, 1979).

The Meaning of Soul Community

Honoring elders as we have described needs a context. This context is the local congregation and its particular way of being a people of God in the world. The way of being a people of God for the local African American congregation is referred to here as the soul community. The concept of soul community attempts to capture the unique qualities of African American Christian congregations that are not found in other Christian congregations.

The communal concept of soul carries a connotation somewhat different from the more widespread individualized understanding of soul, but it is an important aspect of the African American style of life in general and the African American congregation's way of being a people of God in particular.

As a broad concept, soul is understood as the identifiable idiosyncratic character of African American life. It is shaped by the experiences of African Americans and expressed in their everyday life. The character of soul is also multifaceted. Its content is variously described in terms of three main qualities: the creative expressiveness, theology, and solidarity of black people.

In *Roots of Soul,* Alfred B. Pasteur and Ivory L. Toldson (1982) describe soul as the creative expressiveness of black people that enriches life. Creative expressiveness encompasses the spontaneity, emotion, unique rhythms, tones, and representation of life found in African American music, dance, poetry, drama, oratory, folklore, painting, and sculpture. And it is a quality found in food preparation and styling and in the way African Americans express their individuality in such things as clothes and hairstyles.

Henry Mitchell and Nicholas Cooper Lewter titled their book *Soul Theology* (1986). They assert that soul theology comprises core religious beliefs that African Americans hold that nourish and sustain them. Although these beliefs are not unique when viewed separately, they are unique when taken together as a whole. They reflect a unique way of looking at the world that characterizes African Americans and their biblical faith.

In the book *Soulside,* Ulf Hannerz (1969) refers to black soul as an ethos of solidarity. The quality of soul refers to the understanding of a collective identity or peoplehood of African Americans within which is found a shared perspective that he characterizes as soul. His understanding of soul reflects the language that is often used by African Americans, particularly such expressions as "sister" or "brother" in referring to peers who are not blood relatives and "auntie" or "uncle" for elders who are not kin. Language usage is meant to convey African Americans' self-understanding as family members in community and a loyalty to one another that evolved out of a common ethnic and cultural heritage and out of a creative response to external oppression in a hostile environment.

Of great significance is the fact that all three of these dimensions of soul are found in the African American church. That is why we call a local congregation a soul community. Worship in this community is typified by spontaneity, emotion, and upbeat rhythm. Local congregations are sustained by core beliefs that they deem important enough to pass on from one generation to the next. These core beliefs form a soul theology that emerges out of communal experiences with God, whose presence they sense even in their experiences of oppression.

The African American church also historically functioned as an instrument of solidarity in the midst of alienating and divisive forces. It has continued to be a place where individuals are connected, supported, sustained, healed, and loved despite the meanness of life. In the local congregation, persons find a common identity and relational ties for maintaining their spiritual, emotional, physical, and interpersonal well-being. Local congregations as soul communities are indeed forces for solidarity and uplift for African Americans.

In this book, we will place particular emphasis on the communal solidarity of local congregations as the essential context for honoring elders. This context underscores the local congregation as a support system for helping elders and others maintain spiritual, emotional, physical, and interpersonal integrity despite hostile external forces, life transitions, and familial tensions and threats. The context also accentuates the core beliefs and expressive styles of African Americans as important dimensions for responding to the needs of elders and others. Most especially, the focus on the context of honoring will highlight the values and ethical principles drawn from biblical scriptures and African teachings that have informed African American respect for elders and their place in the community. The key value is that respect for elders not only benefits elders but also contributes to the solidarity of the soul community, which ensures the meaningful survival of present and future generations. Honoring elders is not done at the expense of children and young people; on the contrary, it is essential for their well-being and vitality.

Compelling Issues in the Reenvisioning Process

Reenvisioning ministries designed to honor elders requires attention to a number of compelling issues to which these ministries must respond. Of particular urgency is the prevailing and deepening view among churches and clergy alike that the future of churches is built solely around the vitality of youth and young adults. Because of this view, it is difficult for churches and clergy to conceive of how older adults can contribute to the present and future vitality of the entire church community. The opening case of Rev. X speaks to this view but then moves beyond it to a new way of engaging the roles of elders.

The need for reenvisioning is also confirmed by Lincoln and Mamiya (1990). They found that the numerical growth of senior adults in African American churches is being paralleled in a number of instances by a decrease in the interest of the young in the life of the church. Hilliard (1995) also draws attention to the problem of the disintegration of a sense of solidarity or peoplehood. He states, "Pure and simple, we have reached a point in our history where we have been socialized to see ourselves as individuals and cultural neuters. We socialize our children to be the same way. As we become more and more isolated, alone, and culturally undefined, we lose the capacity to see group problems. Gradually the sense of belonging diminishes for so many of us, so that there is hardly an 'us' at all" (p. 131).

This separation about which Lincoln and Mamiya and Hilliard write challenges churches to confront the seeming erosion of the historical environment, defined here as a soul community, wherein a whole community is in solidarity. It also challenges churches to avoid any truncation of the doing and receiving roles of elders that are central to honoring them as well as central to the nature of the soul community.

In short, one of the most compelling reasons for reenvisioning ministries through which elders are honored in an actual soul community is the critical need to recapture the generational ties. Through these ties, elders must assume an indefatigable role that makes possible cultural and historical grounding of the younger generations. Through these ties, the younger generations are enabled to see elders as models of their own journey ahead and of the changes that must be made to improve the quality of life for present and future elders. This is the basis for the kind of solidarity that defines the soul community and that makes honoring elders possible. Conscious attention to this concern in the reenvisioning process is, to use Hilliard's words, "a matter of survival and a matter of meaning" (1995, p. 69).

A second area of urgent need regards the very real fact that we are experiencing in churches, as in the larger society, a fast-growing population of African Americans aged sixty-five and above. Between 1970 and 1980, the number of African Americans aged sixty-five and over in the United States increased by 34 percent (American

Society on Aging, 1992, p. 1). In 1980, older African Americans represented 6.6 percent of the older population. By 1990, this proportion was 8 percent. From 1990 to 2030, the proportion of African Americans aged sixty-five and over is expected to increase by 160 percent (American Association of Retired Persons and the Administration on Aging, 1993, p. 2).

The proportion of older adults in churches is also high. Overall, about one-third of church members are older adults aged sixty-five and over (American Association of Retired Persons, 1993b, p. 3). No hard statistical data exist on numbers of older members in African American churches. However, denominational leaders at the Interdenominational Theological Center estimate that in some churches, the proportion may be consistent with overall church statistics, but in many more churches, the proportion of African American elders is 45 percent or more.

Elders are also spread across metropolitan areas, small towns, and rural areas, although the greatest concentrations are in central-city areas. The challenge to churches is to reenvision ways of maintaining contact with the increasing numbers of aging participants and responding adequately to their needs to be doers and receivers. Certainly, in this regard, churches will need to be particularly alert to elders who, for a variety of reasons, cannot maintain attendance and active participation in congregational life. Research confirms that the frequency of elders' attendance in church tends to be a critical indicator of how often churches provide assistance and how much assistance they give (Taylor, 1988).

A third critical area deals with the economic situation of older African Americans. In 1992, one-third of elderly African Americans lived in poverty, compared to 11 percent of elderly whites (American Association of Retired Persons and the Administration on Aging, 1993, p. 10). Many, particularly women, face continual financial insufficiencies. In fact, the great majority (62 percent) of African American women live in poverty (National Council of Negro Women and National Eldercare Institute, 1992).

Although some elders receive financial help from family members and forms of support from churches, life is not easy for elders who live in poverty or on the borderline. The higher educational attainment levels and beneficial employment experiences of some African American elders have placed them in a relatively secure economic position. However, youth who are recent school dropouts and whose ongoing economic sufficiency is called into question face economic uncertainty as they move toward their elder years. The challenge for churches is to be alert and sensitive to the economic realities faced by both present and future elders and to find ways of responding to these realities.

The family is a fourth compelling area in the reenvisioning process. African American elders are typically portrayed as being an integral part of family life. They perform key advisory functions, and many, particularly women, are caregivers for minor grandchildren and other relatives (Chatters, 1988). Indeed, the grandparent role has become an increasingly salient one for elderly African Americans. Though women typically assume this role, research has shown that grandparenting is a more pivotal role for African American men than for those in other ethnic groups (Pruchno and Johnson, 1996).

Elderly African Americans are more likely then elderly whites to live in extended family households and to reside with children and grandchildren. Likewise, African American elders, particularly spouseless elders, are more likely to have children living with them (Taylor, 1988). At the same time, it must be remembered that households also consist of married elderly couples who reside apart from other family relations. Research also shows that an increasing number of widowed elders over seventy-five years of age are living alone. More of these are widows than widowers (Smith, 1991).

Because more people are living longer, the number of elders in the eighty-five-and-over age category is increasing. This reality is of special significance because this group of elders is most likely to experience dependence on others (Schmall and Pratt, 1989). Persons in this group constitute the truly vulnerable elders. The need to provide long-term care is greatest among these elders. Family decisions about appropriate courses of action are seldom easy; and when family members assume the role of caregiver, there is the potential for strain. Although an appreciable number of elders in this group reside in nursing homes, African American families tend to resist placing elderly relatives in such institutions.

Families also face transitions of their elderly members not simply from health to impairment but also from life-threatening conditions that require critical decisions to death. These transitions and conditions are traumatic; they require special supportive care for elders and family members alike.

A fifth compelling area of concern regards the health of African American elders. Research indicates that these elders experience more health problems and less access to services than older whites do. Moreover, some past gains have been lost (Dorfman, 1991). African American elders are much more likely to rate their health fair or poor compared to elderly whites and are at greater risk for both acute and chronic ailments. Moreover, they experience a greater number of days on which usual activities are restricted due to illness or injury than white elders do (American Association of Retired Persons and the Administration on Aging, 1993). Many, particularly women, face continuing financial insufficiencies. As mentioned earlier, nearly two out of three African American women live in poverty. And an increasing number of widowed African American elders over seventy-five years of age are living alone: 84 percent of African American widows and 65 percent of widowers (Smith, 1991, p. 59). Some elders reside in nursing homes, an increasing number reside with adult children or other relatives, and an appreciable number of grandparents are the sole caregivers for grandchildren.

These realities point up the urgency of an African American community response based on a renewed vision of honoring our elders. African American churches remain important contexts for leading this response. These churches have served and continue to serve as socioemotional and instrumental systems of support for older adults. But how can this reenvisioning be done? An important starting point is revisiting the African American traditional understanding of the expression of honor in the community.

Launching the Reenvisioning Process

It is imperative that our church constituencies reenvision the historical African American understanding of honoring our elders. In doing so, we are called to reenvision our relationships with our elders in the manner in which Thomas Moore (1994) describes relationships, as truly sacred—not in the superficial sense of their simply being valued but in the sense of their calling upon infinite and mysterious depths in ourselves, in our communities, and in the very nature of things. To do this means developing a soul community. Such a community goes beyond the simple mechanics of relating to our elders; indeed, it entails living out our relationships with our elders willingly and lovingly.

Developing the soul community within which honoring our elders is to occur necessitates our tapping the roots of our community found in our African cultural and Judeo-Christian religious heritage. This means that we cannot enter into deep, loving relationships that honor our elders without knowing and appreciating the rich cultural and religious heritage that can empower and nourish those relationships.

Another step involves developing an understanding of various dynamics of relating to older adults in ways that honor them. That is, our ability to honor elders within the context of the soul community depends in part on how we understand our own unfolding life cycle. It also depends on paying attention to the importance we attach to cross-generational relationships and how we actually relate cross-generationally.

Our concern for relational dynamics needs to be followed by envisioning concrete ministry initiatives that respond to the needs of older African American adults and the contemporary issues that older adults and their families face. This also includes ways of assuring that ministries with older adults focus on the three R's of honoring them. Finally, our task in our churches is to discover and attentively nourish ways of responding to our elders' needs and their right to a place in the soul community. This means that we must be concerned that the elders are part of the deliberations that affect their lives and that there is an environment for them and family members to grapple with ethical decisions surrounding life and death.

Questions for Reflection

1. What evidence of honoring elders do you see in your church? Where is change needed in how honor is understood and carried out in your church?

2. How does your church exemplify the soul community and its importance for honoring elders?

3. What is the situation of older adults in your family, church, and community? In which of their struggles can the church give assistance?

4. What examples can you cite of older adults as recipients of care, repositories of wisdom, and resourceful contributors to community? How does your church community show that these roles of elders are valued?

2

TAPPING OUR ROOTS

AFRICAN AND BIBLICAL
TEACHINGS ABOUT ELDERS

Temba L. J. Mafico

DAVIS OCRAN, A FORTY-THREE-YEAR-OLD MAN from Effiduasi Ashanti in Ghana, West Africa, tells of a tradition of honoring elders that survives to this day. The tradition holds that the oldest person is the one to be most respected. The oldest person is given the right to oversee and administer justice. The elder makes decisions to which the young must adhere. It is understood that wisdom comes with age. Because of the authority given to persons of wisdom, a younger person cannot speak until permitted by an elder, regardless of the ideas the younger person may have.

"Even today," Ocran notes, "there is a council of elders made up of heads of families who are scattered about. The council meets during times of crisis, including on issues pertaining to the care of elders and funerals. I am part of that council. But I cannot speak so long as someone older than I is present. I am allowed to speak only when that person permits me to do so. So even now, elders, by virtue of their age, have rights that younger persons cannot usurp.

"But the important point," he continues, "is that respect of elders holds the society together. Our elders' experiences in life make them authorized teachers of our history and traditions. They are the communicators of the wisdom of the people to the younger generations.

They are the *griots,* or storytellers. The whole society is dependent
on their being able to teach us through the stories they tell. The
Bible tells us that a people without a vision will perish. In my culture, we also believe that a people without elders will perish" (Davis
Ocran, personal interview, 1996).

o

Honoring elders is a significant part of the African American religious
heritage. So also is the soul community as the context of solidarity for
expressing honor. We find these roots in our ancestral African home-
land and in our Judeo-Christian tradition. The opening story told by
Davis Ocran introduces us to some aspects of this heritage we still
find today on his and my own native continent of Africa. Ocran's and
my roots and the roots of African American Christians also lie in the
abundance of teachings and exhortations found in Scripture.

The Importance of Tapping Our Roots

Michael Dyson (1993) reminds us that recalling our roots is an ethical imperative. When we remember our traditions, we tap into some
deep truths about life that are instrumental to our survival. In fact,
by connecting with our heritage, we discover anew rich images that
are paradigmatic of what we want to consider for ministry with and
on behalf of elders today and in the future. These images remind us
of the meaning of honoring our elders. They guide us in honoring elders within a soul community focused on our being with them, valuing them, and assuring their place as community contributors and
receivers of care. They suggest approaches to ministry with and on
behalf of our elders that are worthy of a perpetual legacy.

   We need desperately to be influenced by these images in contemporary society, where we all too easily embrace individualistic values, generational rather than cross-generational connections, and a
youth orientation. Of course, we must be willing to acknowledge the
presence and negative impact of current societal values. If we do
not, we will fail to see the significance of our heritage values.

Facing Individualistic and Generational Orientations

African American congregations have not been immune to the influence of individualistic values found in the wider social sphere. Nor
have our congregations been untouched by the emphasis on genera-

tional versus cross-generational relationships. A congregation falls prey to individualistic values when it becomes ingrown and fails to reach out to support and nurture the extended family in the everyday community. When this happens, it fails to acknowledge and honor elders beyond its doors and beyond its participants. The congregation becomes an "individualized agency" that has lost the communal strategy of our heritage.

A congregation also falls prey to individualistic values when individuals within it ignore the common good by denying the contribution and need of elders in the shared communal space. When this happens, the congregation becomes a haven of individualized groups whose actions belie the solidarity emphasis in our heritage.

Congregational programming also reflects separate age-related divisions, particularly in church schools and "children's church." Although important, these divisions often reflect greater concern for their own existence than for intergenerational activity. When this happens, the congregation functions as individualized age-segregated units that militate against the sense of peoplehood so pronounced in our heritage. As a result, in many instances, we see a widening gap between older adults and persons at younger ages and stages.

We fall short if a congregation fails to be a whole community devoted to intentional efforts at human connectedness. We honor elders when we include them as part of this connectedness within and beyond our congregations. We pay homage to our heritage when we build a foundation for a ministry of honoring elders from that heritage.

Facing the Prevailing Youth Orientation

A problem I have seen in the Western world is its dominant youth orientation, which has resulted in a preoccupation with shielding one's true age as one grows older. A story told by a colleague reflects this orientation:

> During my weekly visits to several residents of a nursing home, one of the residents told me about a women's group to which she belonged for a number of years. She enjoyed the group immensely and rarely missed a meeting. The group socialized, did service projects, and had meals together. But there was one activity that was always uncomfortable for her. They celebrated birthdays, and as part of the celebration around the meal table,

the "birthday gal" was always asked to announce her age. This was something that my nursing home pal simply would not do because she did not want anyone to know she was "getting on in years." She felt that her age was no one's business and ought not have any impact on the lives of anyone else.

To get around telling her age, this woman would stuff something into her mouth so that whatever she pretended to say would be wholly unintelligible. After many such occurrences, the other women finally demanded that she "come clean," and they did it at a time when she had no food to place in her mouth. She recalled: "I told them that a long time ago, I had purchased an ornate chest. Each of the drawers had a lock and key. At one point, I decided to put my age inside one of the drawers. I locked it inside and forgot about it. I have since lost the key, and to this day, I can't remember where it is or what my age is."

Adults tend to be bothered by birthdays. They are acutely aware that they are aging by virtue of their advancing chronological age, and they tend to try very hard to keep their age a secret from others in the community. African Americans have adopted this manner of negating their aging process, and by so doing, they place in question their own and others' positive being and becoming senior adults in the community.

Anne Wimberly has already stated in Chapter One that in this youth-oriented culture, our churches tend to emphasize the importance of youth to its vitality and future. They also tend to emphasize the need for youth programming, which, typically, isolates youth from the larger intergenerational context that includes elders. It is not surprising, then, that many of our youth do not care to be around elders and do not feel that elders have much to contribute to their well-being. We need desperately to reconnect with our cultural and biblical roots for the guidance they can give us.

It is important for us to consider anew both our African heritage and our Judeo-Christian roots and, in so doing, reflect on how we and others in our churches regard elders today. We want our consideration of these roots to help us move away from our propensity to view aging and being old as unacceptable and toward our looking at aging and older adulthood as indispensable to the life of the community. Moreover, it is important for us to reclaim these roots because of the potential they hold for enhancing our understanding of ministries that honor our elders.

An African American cultural and biblical perspective on aging and older adulthood in the context of community is the topic for our consideration in the remaining sections of this chapter. To consider this topic, we will explore the African and biblical views as parallel views. Throughout our exploration, we will keep in mind that the two views have parallel characteristics. Thus if we understand the African view of aging and older adulthood in the context of community, we will be able to appreciate Old and New Testament ways of looking at them as well. The dominant characteristics that define the parallel views on aging and older adulthood have to do with an orientation to life in the community. It is to this orientation that we now turn.

African and Biblical Orientation to Life

African and biblical views on aging and older adulthood reflect an orientation to life that differs in some important ways from the contemporary Western one. Depicted in Figure 2.1, the contemporary view embraces the *linear life of individuals*. According to the linear view, life moves through an unfolding series of changes or temporal transitions that are informed by biological, social, and cultural dimensions (Tatenhove, 1995; Clements, 1995; Hultsch and Deutsch, 1981). Figure 2.1 shows that we are born at point A and move in linear fashion to point B, which is death. In this model, birthdays move people closer and closer to the grave. At the end of life, we raise the question of whether we have successfully completed certain life tasks or developed essential behavioral capacities. We make sense of our lives or arrive at meaning on this basis. Moreover, in the linear model, what comes after point B is unknown, unless we draw on beliefs about the hereafter.

What I have observed in our youth-oriented society is that as persons perceive their movement toward the end point, they are regarded as "over the hill." I have observed the impact of this model on persons as young as twenty-five years of age, who believe that they are already past their prime in life. Moreover, as persons proceed through retirement, many feel that they have been "put out to pasture." However, the African and biblical Hebrew orientation to life differs markedly from the contemporary model. Let us consider, first, the African orientation.

African Orientation to Life

Africans embrace a view of *circular life in community*. Shown in Figure 2.2, this orientation is part of the overarching circular view of traditional extended family life in Africa.

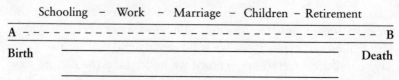

Figure 2.1. Western Linear Life of Individuals.

In Africa, the events of life, the form of families, and the relation-ships of extended family members to one another are expressed as circles. Circles also serve as ongoing reminders of the qualities of in-terdependence, unity, humility, and the absence of greed that perme-ate community life (Mbiti, 1990; Diallo and Hall, 1989; Staples and Johnson, 1993).

In the circular view, life events accentuate the rhythm of commu-nity life. The primary life events of birth, adolescent rites of passage, marriage and child rearing, and death are processes that connect members in the kinship circle. They also connect the living with the departed, or "living dead," who remain alive in the memories of sur-viving families. Consequently, event A, the birth of a child, is the concern not simply of the immediate family but of everyone in the community including the elders and the living dead. The child owes its existence to the existence of the elders and the departed and is ev-idence of the circularity of life (Mbiti, 1990).

The adolescent rites of passage that comprise event B mark the entry of young people between the ages of thirteen and sixteen into adult life. As part of the rites, the initiates form a miniature commu-nity in which they play the role of the elders in order to internalize the significance of honoring and respecting older people. Persons continue around the circle to event C, marriage and child rearing, whereby people pass on the heritage begun by the ancestors and passed along by the elders. Then the process of life moves on around the circle to the moment of physical death when the person becomes one of the living dead (Mbiti, 1990).

Africans celebrate these events as pivotal markers in the circular-ity of time. In this circular conception of time, movement into elder-hood and death is not the end. This movement leads back to event A, birth. Certain tribes of West Africa believe that a dead person is reborn as a baby. Many others believe that when old people die, they become ancestors who continue to associate with and influence the affairs of the living.

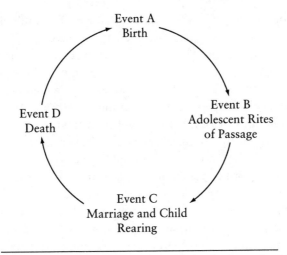

Figure 2.2. African Circular Life in Community.

Thus life does not end with death, for people continue living as ancestors. And their status as ancestors is a highly respected position because they are regarded as stronger than when they were alive in the flesh. They are no longer limited by physicality. They can now go anywhere—to Africa, America, and elsewhere—to see their kinfolk without the restriction of the body. Just as they were wholly part of the community in the flesh and experienced the community's celebration of life events, so now they are acknowledged by the community as ancestors who continue to be part of the life of the community.

Consequently, in the paradigm of circular life, persons are never alone. They are always part of the community. And they know that they in turn need the community. This is, in fact, the meaning of the African proverb, "I am because we are; and because we are, I am." This proverb encapsulates the understanding that my identity shines only as part of the whole. The whole includes everyone—young and old, living and dead.

Biblical Orientation to Life

In many respects, the Old Testament orientation to life is similar to the African. The Old Testament emphasizes what is known as the corporate personality. In this view, as in the African model of circular life in community, persons cannot be alone. The individual exists with others and knows the self to be part of the community. And to feel secure, happy, and whole, a person must be in a cycle that is accepted, supported, and honored by the community. Thus the ancient Hebrews always understood the self as being in a community and as concerned with the people. This community, these people, included not only the present generation who live in the flesh but also ancestors who have died. Indeed, the ancient Hebrews understood that the experiences of their ancestors informed their common life and unfolding story. Former generations helped to fashion the soul of the people and of the family by how they lived their lives in relation to one another and to God. Thus the ancient Hebrews saw ancestors as indispensible to the formation of a psychically or spiritually felt communal whole, and as the source of succeeding generations' recognition of their soul (Pedersen, 1964, p. 474).

An example of the corporate nature of the Hebrew personality is contained in the confession of a descendant of Jacob found in Deuteronomy 26:5–10a. In this passage, the confessor identifies "a wandering Aramaean" as his own ancestor and shares, briefly, the plot of this ancestor's story. The confessor then merges his personal self with the ancestral nation, their particular experiences of oppression, and their release from it, thus claiming their story and God's presence in it as his own. Finally, his sharing in what happened to a former generation and his regarding of their story as his own resulted in his envisioning his role in the present community.

The important point is the confessor's realization that the personal self, the forebears, the ancestral community, and the present community comprised a whole people. Moreover, this whole people was connected to God, who acted in the lives of a whole people, thereby engendering the personal response of the confessor.

A related Old Testament pattern that discloses the corporate personality is the connection of individuals and successive generations through genealogical lists, or genealogical trees, as they are sometimes called. Nearly two dozen such lists appear in the Old Testament. The first appears in Genesis 4:17–22 (from Cain through seven generations). The most extensive is found in 1 Chronicles 1:1–9:44 (from Adam to the descendants of Saul). Through such recounted genealogies, individuals and the contents of their lives live on as part of the psychic community. More than this, however, the genealogical tree serves as a metaphor for the common life of the family, which grows and spreads through the individual shoots it constantly sends forth. Just as the tree's branch owes its existence to the trunk and the root, receiving nourishment from them, the individual person is nourished only in connection with his or her family (Pedersen, 1964, pp. 257, 267).

In sum, the Old Testament confession and the genealogies highlight the nature of the corporate personality paradigm, in which there is an ongoing connection between "I" and "we," as shown in Figure 2.3. Importantly, the substance of this paradigm parallels the meaning of the African proverb, "I am because we are; and because we are, I am."

Persons are also honored to reach old age in the community before dying and becoming part of the ancestral community. In Genesis 25:8–9, for example, it is written: "Abraham breathed his last and died in a good old age, an old man and full of years, and was gathered to his people. His sons Isaac and Ishmael buried him in the cave of Machpelah."

We should notice that Abraham's advanced age is positively described as "a good old age." The other way the Israelites described Abraham's very advanced age is that "he was an old man full of years." He lived the full cycle of life, and it was understood that the number of years a person lives is a gift of God. This positive

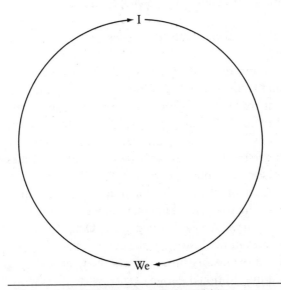

Figure 2.3. Elderhood and the Old Testament Corporate Personality.

description of aging is also repeated in Job 42:17: "And Job died, an old man, and full of days."

The Role of Elders in the Community

In the opening story, we learned about the revered status of elders in Davis Ocran's home country in West Africa. This same veneration of elders pervades Chipinga, the district of Zimbabwe where I was born. We also believe that the greatest teacher of all is experience acquired through the years. When I became a pastor at a very early age, I was asked to chair a meeting at which everyone was older than I. Though I had the knowledge to run the church and had received more schooling than my church members, I did not have as much experience of life as they had. One elderly man with whom I was disagreeing touched his gray hair and told me that he was "not gray as a joke." In other words, I was arguing from what I had learned, whereas the elder was arguing from tested knowledge acquired through experience.

Old age conferred high status among both the African and the Hebrew peoples. Older persons were important participants in the African community and in the Hebrew community. They held certain positions and roles and received respect because of their longevity and their community participation.

Traditional and Contemporary Roles

The prayer of a traditional African was to live a long life. One major distinguishing factor between traditional Africans and contemporary people is that traditional Africans did not fear aging. Every old person desired to be the oldest person still living. In the past, as today, old age accords a person significant status in the community. An old person is understood as having experienced the vicissitudes of life. It is for this reason that young people consult them for advice.

The oldest person alive in the community can remember the way things were in the past. An old person may therefore be regarded as the "living library." As we learned from Ocran's story, the elders were the keepers of the history of the community; they were the *griots* who passed the history on to the next generation.

Elderhood in traditional Africa carried with it a responsibility for the young. The elderly played with the grandchildren when their parents were at work or on a journey. They preoccupied the children's minds with tales they told and with songs they taught. Most of the stories and songs the children would remember into their own old age and pass on to their own grandchildren. The grandparents acted as counselors to young people in matters of marriage and child rearing, and they motivated the young people to aim high in setting their life objectives.

It was understood that the elders had an important role to play with young people during one of the most difficult times in life, the period between childhood and adulthood. Africans addressed the need of the young during this period to find their identity by guiding them through the rites of passage. Adults, especially the elders, were central figures in this process.

The role of the elders was to help the young through the transition from youth to adulthood. The elders undertook this role with intentionality. Young people did not become adults by accident or simply by evolution or an unconscious sort of "growing up." I experienced this role of the elders in my own family.

There are thirteen children in my family, eight boys and five girls. All of us are now married and have families of our own. Although I now live in the United States, my siblings all live in cities scattered throughout Zimbabwe. Whenever the parents of one of the families in Zimbabwe want to go on a distant trip, they take the children and leave them with my parents. One time my mother, at age seventy-nine, was caring for fifteen children.

The children are active, as children always are. Some may be fighting, others crying for food, and some calling for their grandmother's attention. They keep my mother busy keeping the peace, feeding babies, carrying babies. She loves it, and the children do too. My father sits on the veranda with the older children telling stories of our heritage. Most of the stories have a moral lesson. Thus my parents serve as nursery, kindergarten, and school. They are the nurturers and the teachers. They are true grandparents to their grandchildren because they are more experienced than the children's parents. They are the ones who know and guide the process analogous to the transformation described in 1 Corinthians 13:11: "When I was a child, I reasoned like a child; when I became an adult, I put an end to childish ways."

In short, we see in the traditional African community the contribution of the elders to community life and the honor shown them by the community's recognition of their contribution. This heritage offers an essential foundation for the contemporary ministry mentioned in

Chapter One that includes elders as repositories of wisdom and resourceful contributors to community life.

The young also had responsibility for the elders. The old could
expect to be rejuvenated by the young people's vibrancy, jokes, talk,
and even behavior. Young people gave the elders a cause and a willingness to affirm life. Young people kept them from depression that
could result from loneliness and inactivity. Grandchildren helped
grandparents exercise their bodies. In fact, respect shown and care
given to the oldest persons alive in a community were the assumed
responses of all who had not reached that status. This reality of traditional African communal life is fundamental to the contemporary
ministry mentioned in Chapter One that emphasizes elders as recipients of care.

The Role of Elders Among the Israelites

Parallels exist between the roles of elders in African life and the roles
of elders among the Old Testament Israelites. As righteous followers
of God, elders were considered an asset to the community as noted
in Psalm 92:12–15: "The righteous flourish like the palm tree, and
grow like a cedar in Lebanon. They are planted in the house of the
Lord; they flourish in the courts of God. In old age they still produce
fruit; they are always green and full of sap, showing that the Lord is
upright; he is my rock, and there is no unrighteousness in him." This
passage illuminates our understanding that the gift of life is from
God and that elders are enabled to respond to God's blessing
through their presence and participation in the community.

As in African life, old age was also a badge of honor among the
Israelites. Evidence of this appears in Genesis. Joseph's brothers had
come to Egypt to buy food. They did not know that the merchant
they were dealing with was Joseph; Joseph realized who they were
but said nothing. At one point, Joseph asked them, "Is your father
well, the old man of whom you spoke? Is he still alive?" (Gen.
43:27). This question about Jacob, his father too, is significant.
Joseph is concerned with the well-being of the old man; he wants to
know whether he is still alive and well. But it was also wholly appropriate that he inquire after the health of the head of his cus-
tomers' family.

It is noteworthy that Jacob is still the head of the family in spite
of his advanced years. It is he who sends Joseph's brothers to Egypt
to buy grain (Gen. 42:1–2, 43:1–2). He is the patriarch of the fam-

ily, and his word is greatly respected by his adult married sons. For their part, they will try by all means to please their father by doing his will. Age has given Jacob great status. Certain positions and roles were performed according to one's age. When Joseph prepared a banquet for his brothers, he sat them around the table according to their age.

Old Testament tradition also shows that a close relationship existed between the elders $(Z^eq\bar{e}n\hat{i}m)$ and youth $(y^el\bar{a}d\hat{i}m)$, as noted in the following passages in Proverbs: "Grandchildren are the crown of the aged, and the glory of children is their parents" (Prov. 17:6). "The glory of the young is their strength, but the beauty of the aged is their gray hair" (Prov. 20:29). These passages highlight the mutual benefit of the association between the young and the old. For the Israelites, the young were the deepest joys of the elders, and they saw the young as their responsibility to correct and direct in order that they develop into persons of uprightness and integrity. Gray hair was also a sign of seniority and wisdom in Old Testament times. Thus young people, by their association with old people, benefited from the elders' wisdom. And the members of the older generation are reminded of their past vibrancy, which they see in the youth. It is this reason, more than any other I can think of, that makes grandparents and grandchildren ideal friends and playmates.

As in the African community, the Israelites addressed the need of the young for guidance in the transition from childhood to adulthood through the bar mitzvah ceremony for boys. This ceremony continues today. The corresponding ceremony for girls, the bat mitzvah, was invented a century ago in the reform branch of Judaism, which is primarily American. As in the African rites of passage, the relatives, uncles, grandparents, friends, and community surround the young person and assist the youth in claiming identity as an adult. The role of elders is crucial.

Another component of persons' attitudes toward individuals older than themselves is found in the Ten Commandments. God's fifth command was for children, at whatever age, to honor their parents. And honoring them had the promise of longevity for the one who honored: "Honor your father and your mother, so that your days may be long in the land that the Lord your God is giving you" (Exod. 20:12).

Honor of elders also meant showing concern for the plight of widows. Indeed, it was understood in Old Testament times that neglecting to do so provoked God's wrath (Deut. 14:29, 27:19; Isa. 1:16–17).

The concern for widows was also carried over into the early Christian church. The Christian community took steps to provide for widows' needs (Acts 6:1–6) and advised families to care for their own (1 Tim. 5:3–4, 16). Moreover, several New Testament sayings emphasize honoring parents, thereby supporting Old Testament Jewish views (Matt. 19:19a; Luke 18:20b; Mark 10:19b).

We also find in the New Testament the exemplary role of older adults in the life of the community. One such elder was Anna, whose exemplary role is described in the Gospel of Luke: "There was also a prophet, Anna, the daughter of Phanuel, of the tribe of Asher. She was of a great age, having lived with her husband seven years after her marriage, then as a widow to the age of eighty-four. She never left the temple but worshiped there with fasting and prayer night and day. At that moment she came, and began to praise God and to speak about the child to all who were looking for the redemption of Jerusalem" (Luke 2:36–38).

The significance of Anna as an elder is her faithfulness as a worshiper at the temple and in her personal life of devotion. Her age was not a barrier to her participation in the community, her consciousness of what was going on around her, or her spiritual understanding that allowed her to perceive who Jesus was. By her example, she carries on the tradition of Abraham, Moses, and David, elderly leaders and exemplars of faithful service to God in Old Testament Israel (Gilmore, 1992).

Concluding Commentary

Old age was cherished in biblical times because it is a gift denied many. The elders have qualities and attributes that make them indispensable advisers, storytellers, historians, and spiritual leaders in the community. In African tradition, elderly people were a resource from whom the younger generations obtained historical information, advice, experience, and tender care. In both biblical times and in Africa, old age was a status symbol. People enjoyed being old because age was not associated with weakness, uselessness in the community, or dependence on the children or the state. Rather, old age brought wisdom based on experience. Elders were honored and accorded respect by the younger generations in recognition of their significant community service. Thus both older and younger generations had roles to play in the community. The elders felt loved and continued to make their contributions to the community.

Questions for Reflection

1. What are your attitudes toward aging and older adulthood? How do members in your church view aging and older adulthood?

2. What roles do older adults play in your family and church? How do elders and youth relate to each other? What examples of the roles described in this chapter can you identify in your family and church?

3. How might your family and church promote ongoing positive attitudes toward older adults?

4. How might you, your family, and your church promote positive relationships between older adults and the younger generations?

THE CHURCH AS A
SOUL COMMUNITY

Anne Streaty Wimberly

A GROUP OF OLDER AFRICAN AMERICANS was asked to describe a church that may be called a soul community, the importance of this community in their lives, and what it means to honor elders in it. One elderly woman gave the following detailed response:

"I don't know what the church as a soul community means to anybody else. But the way I look at it, any church that has 'soul' is an alive church. Let me tell you what I mean. As long as I can remember, the church has been part of my life and I've been part of the church's life. You know, the only way I can think about my church is to think of it as family. When a church is like a family, it's alive. Now, I'm not saying we're a perfect family. Far from it. I can remember some pretty serious disagreements along the way. But my church is where I always felt like I belonged. It's been an anchor for me. It still is. I sang in the choir, I went to Sunday school, and I belong to the women's group even now, though I don't always get to meetings anymore. You know, you feel like you're honored when you belong somewhere—I mean, really belong where others accept you, love you, care about you, and know that you have something of the same to give to them.

"The church is where I knew everybody and everybody knew me. I guess you'd say we all grew up together. We prayed together. We played together. We were there for one another's children. We did what we could when somebody was sick or in trouble and when somebody died. We made lifelong friends that after a while we thought of as family. And we didn't just keep it in the church. We really did try to help people in and outside the church. I guess you'd say our soul was in it. Because of that, the church was a beacon in our community. It was an alive church. Its life showed from the inside out. It was the kind of soul you just couldn't hide.

"A lot of people who came along during the same time I did are dead now. So is my husband. I've been a widow many years now. I still think of the church as family. But things are different now. I don't get there as often as I used to. It's not so easy to get around anymore. I go when I can. The pastor comes to see me and brings a church bulletin and a tape of the service when I'm absent. I get visits from others, too. I'm grateful for that. I try to do what I can, though. I mean, I give what I can, and I try to send cards to people on the sick and shut-in list.

"Is it important for the church to be a soul community? Is honoring important? Yes, yes! It's important for young folk and us old folk to honor one another. Nobody wants to be left by the wayside. I know I don't, yet sometimes now I fear it will happen. But the main thing is, if the church is going to be like a family, people sure have to have their soul in it. I mean, they have to want it that way deep down inside, and they have to believe deep down inside that God wants it that way. And if we believe it, we have to act like it and mean it from the heart. And one more thing. You can't have soul without honor. That's what I think."

○

Knowing what a soul community is and how we form it is fundamental for Christian ministry that honors elders. We have already introduced the soul community as the church that operates from a sense of peoplehood where we intend to assure the place of elders as contributors and receivers of care. The opening story in this chapter also calls attention to a similar view of its meaning held by elders.

Our intent in this chapter is to give further attention to its meanings and importance. We will consider in depth what soul community means from an African American Christian viewpoint. We will explore its Christian origins in Scripture. We will also focus on specific aspects of soul relationships, commitment in relationships, and several important habits that authenticate honor-bestowing activity in a Christian community.

Gaining further understanding of its meanings is essential because this kind of community enlivens our honoring efforts. Without it, we fail to honor the elders fully. Indeed, we are reminded by the opening story that the honoring process and the soul environment within which it occurs are inseparable.

Christian Origins of the Soul Community

Soul is a theological concept appearing in Scripture in at least three different forms. One is in the image of the immortal soul. This concept derives from the immortality of believers made possible by an imperishable God and Christ's resurrection (Rom. 1:23; 1 Tim. 1:17; 2 Tim. 1:10; 1 Pet. 11:23; 1 Cor. 15:42, 50, 52–54).

Both the Old and New Testaments give us a second view of soul that goes beyond its immaterial and immortal nature. In this second instance, soul connotes our aliveness as human beings. It characterizes the life principle. It identifies life given by God (Gen. 2:7) and conveys a sense of our human vitality as God's people that comes from our hearts (Deut. 6:5, 10:12–14). It also depicts life in God that involves our yearning for God's guidance (Ps. 119:20), our expression of our emotional selves to God in response to life's journey (Ps. 6:3), and our joyful worship of God and recognition of God's blessings (Ps. 103:1).

The Sociotheological Nature of Soul in Scripture

Scripture also conveys a third image of soul that is distinctly sociotheological. More than the others, this view identifies the character of collective life that gives shape to our understanding of soul community. In this view, soul is the spirit, heart, or character of our being, thinking, and acting in response to God. A concern for relationships is at its center.

Jesus' emphasis on the Great Commandment typifies this relationship and shows the continuity between the Old Testament people of God and the New Testament church. The Great Commandment emphasizes that our life in the community is to portray our love of God with all our heart, soul, mind, and spirit, and to love others as ourselves (Matt. 22:35–40; Mark 12:28–34; Luke 10:25–28). This relational ethic characterized Jesus' consistent concern for the wholeness of the community and all within it. It became not simply the identifying characteristic of the community he sought to establish but the quality of the ministry he modeled. Jesus' ministry was that of responding to the actual experiences of people and the conditions of their lives that demanded care and healing. He spoke about and modeled compassionate friendship that extended to society's outcasts and needy of all ages (Matt. 9:11; Mark 1:29–31, 2:15–17; Luke 7:34, 14:12–14, 15:1–32). And he challenged others to be his friend by their showing friendship to others (John 15:14).

Jesus' followers sought to conform to his image and to follow what he did in the New Testament church after his death and resurrection. In this early church, we see an expansion of the sociotheological view of soul in the representation of the church as a community of solidarity. The Christian community became a new kind of family. It took on the quality of an extended family that went beyond blood ties (Gal. 6:10; Eph. 2:19).

Soul also became incorporated in a particular meaning of communal spirit, or life, and in the virtues of faith, hope, and love that define the inner core of Christian life. First Peter emphasizes the collective life that is represented by "unity of spirit, sympathy, love for one another, a tender heart, and a humble mind" (3:8). The apostle Paul stressed a community wherein members draw closely together and closely to Christ, giving them a deep sense of identity with him and with one another (1 Cor. 12:12–31; Rom. 12:4–8; Eph. 1:22–23, 2:20, 4:15–16; Col. 1:18, 2:19; Achtemeier, 1985). The writer of Hebrews emphasizes a community of remembering who recalled ancestral exemplars of the faith. Remembering was to reinforce the community's identity and sustain it by providing hope-filled reminders of the necessity of an inner core of faith (Heb. 11:1–12:2). First John (4:19) highlights the essential component of respect for others and contributions to their well-being that are born out of love that first came from God.

A Basis for Forming a Soul Community

We find in the images of community in Scripture a paramount sense of the sacredness of persons, of their being gifts from God that make them worthy of honor. These images serve as models for us today in our ministry with and on behalf of elders. But in James Ashbrook's terms (1996), making this community a reality cannot be taught like geography or spelling. And certainly, there is more to it than simply discovering approaches and deciding to respond to the needs of elders.

Forming a community in which we honor elders comes from our willingness to be shaped by images of Jesus Christ, the community he heralded, and the ministry he undertook within it. It also comes from allowing the spirit of God to act in our lives to bring God's purposes about through what we do. We need to be constantly confronted by Scripture because it is central to our being shaped by the image of Jesus Christ and his ministry (Mulholland, 1985).

As African Americans, we also need continually to recall images of community found in our cultural heritage as a means of affirming who we are as a people and practices that are consistent with Scripture. Moreover, we need to hear the elders' past and present experiences in the community and recognize that all of us create and participate in the community in ways that distinguish us as humans. Through what we hear and recognize, we want to see how to join our biblical and cultural heritage and present meaning structures in ways that take seriously the image of Jesus Christ and his ministry. This connecting process also helps us see and envision responses to the challenges before us to develop a culturally relevant yet biblically based community and ministry.

In the following section, we will summarize the connections between our cultural and biblical heritage, contemporaneous views of elders, and the human longing for relationships. We will focus specifically on two key aspects of soul relationships: family and Christian friendship. Our intent is to become aware of the importance of these aspects in churches today and to uncover challenges we face in making these relationships work.

Family and Friendship as Dimensions of Soul Relationships

The biblical and cultural foundations traced by Temba Mafico in Chapter Two and the opening story in this chapter clearly remind us that relationships are important. Mafico described the circularity of relationships in Africa and the "I-we" relationships in the Old Testament, both of which underscored family. The elder's story at the beginning of this chapter places emphasis on belongingness in community made possible by relations with family and friends. New Testament references cited in this chapter also described Christlike and God-empowered family and friendship relationships as constitutive of Christian community.

Taking Family Relations Seriously

We must give serious attention to the concept of family as a defining aspect in what we do to shape a soul community that takes elders into account. One reason is that now, as in their earlier years, elders are inherently social. Like persons at every age and stage of life, they seek caring relationships with others—that is part of being human. Such connections contribute to the elders' abiding sense of self and support a meaningful life. They are arrangements through which we honor elders.

The church is one place where many elders can build and maintain relationships. In addition to what the elder in the opening story said, another elder put it this way: "The church is the main contact some of us have with the outside world. It's where we feel like we're family. Our dearest friends are there."

A second reason is that historically, the church has been a central institution for African Americans of all ages. All relied on the church to be the soul of the community in the midst of oppressive conditions and social crises. This role is reflected in the spiritual sanctuary the church provided and in the special sense of "family kinship" centered on mutual support and individual and communal well-being (Woodson, 1945).

Family kinship within the church also crossed generational lines. This meant that the African American church's concern was for people at every age and stage. As such, the church developed as a resource for responding not simply to the spiritual needs and life issues of the young but also to those of its elders. The church developed as an extended family to elders and as a vital context for coping used by them (Chatters, 1988; Chatters and Taylor, 1989; Taylor, 1988; Taylor and Chatters, 1986, 1989).

Facing Challenges in Forming Family Relations

In our attempt to preserve the kinds of relationships that appear so consistently in our past, in Scripture, and in current elders' stories, we must also be aware of current challenges. This need is underscored by the elderly woman's statement in the opening story that "things are different now." Another elder said, "Any semblance of my church as I once knew it is purely coincidental. Our youngsters have grown up. Many have moved away. New people have come into the church. The music has changed. New songs have replaced the old songs and hymns I love. Some things we do in church are still familiar, but in other things, I feel like a stranger." Still another elder stated, "I know some older people hold onto offices and responsibilities that ought to be passed on to younger folk. But we don't want to be 'put out to pasture' either."

These statements illumine our understanding that human affairs change over time, as do the character and dynamics of the church as family. We also recognize that many older adults have established over time ritualized patterns of relating in the church. They have become accustomed to particular ways of doing things that are familiar to them. This familiarity provides a sense of security that, in essence, holds the self together. What they find familiar is linked to their feelings of familial security or of being coherently connected with others.

It is difficult for many elders to abandon things with which they are familiar and to which they feel connected and devoted without experiencing a sense of loss and anxiety. At the same time, we recognize that new and younger members struggle with the same needs for the familiar and the familial qualities of church. The resulting dilemma is what we call generational conflict or the generation gap. In its dishonoring form, the conflict sometimes results in the young's ostentatious disregard of the elders' standards or their show of indifference to them (Mead, 1970). In its honoring form, we as the church family take to heart the essential needs of elders for both the familiar and the familial qualities of the church. We are also challenged to become aware of the changes in the character and dynamics of the church as family and the church's need to respond to change in ways that foster the biblical understanding of relationships in God's family.

Seeing Christian Friendship as a Soul Relationship

Just as some elders describe caring relationships within the church as a sense of family, others use the image of Christian friendship. In describing one particularly close friendship, an elderly woman said, "I don't know what I would do without my friend. Our friendship started in our church and goes back many, many years. We count on each other for support. Both of us are widows now. We call each other to make sure everything is OK. We pray for each other. We share our concerns about things going on in our lives and keep up on what's going on in the lives of each other's children. We talk about old times, too. We wrestle together with what might yet happen in our lives—our health and the loss of our friendship through death."

In another instance, a middle-aged woman and an elderly woman, who lived a great distance from each other, became telephone prayer partners. They forged a deeply meaningful mutual friendship in their weekly exchanges. They shared the stories of their weekly journey, words of encouragement, and prayers for God's presence, guidance, and sustenance in each other's lives and the lives of loved ones and others in need.

As with church family relationships, the importance of Christian friendship lies in its ability to enrich human life through its unique qualities. In addition to earlier-cited biblical understandings of friendship and elders' comments on it, we recognize that true friendship encompasses qualities of loyalty and steadfastness (Prov. 17:17, 18:24; Eccles. 6:14–16). But the Bible also warns that poverty or adversity often reveals people to be friends in name only (Prov. 19:4, 6–7; Eccles. 12:9, 13:21, 37:4–5). This latter notion about friendship is particularly important today as we note instances where church members distance themselves from elders. It happens because people have negative views of aging, the circumstances of elders prevent their regular attendance, or they have illnesses or debilities that make communication with them difficult. Moreover, we are reminded by the elder's statement in the opening story that as persons grow older, their peer circle shrinks as the people around them die. But the need for and salience of close relationships remains.

Facing Challenges in Forming Friendships

We are challenged in our individualistic society to assure a sense of obligation based on love to support and aid elders as though our very life depends on it. This kind of friendship binds us to one another and to Jesus Christ. Indeed, when we exemplify this kind of friendship, we show our love of Jesus Christ and claim his promised friendship.

We are challenged, too, to discover ways of sharing experiences openly and increasingly with elders. In this way, we make deeper friendships possible and heighten the desire to respond to these elders' needs. In one example, the youth group in a local congregation became friends of homebound elders. One Sunday each month, the young people went to their elder friends' homes to read the Bible, to share experiences, and to pray and sing together. The youth were surprised by their own enjoyment of their relationships with the elders. Because of the meaningfulness of these experiences with their elder friends, the youth developed ongoing motivation to continue these relationships. The number of youth-elder friendships increased.

In sum, we are challenged to develop friendships with elders based on our realization that God values all human beings, including the elders, and the quality of friendship with elders comes from our seeing them through God's eyes. Only in this way do we bring to life the relational quality of soul.

The Necessity of Commitment

We have said that caring relationships define a ministry with elders that honors them and that caring relationships are at the core of soul. Yet relationships without commitment do not go very far. Consequently, it is essential for us to give attention to commitment. Consider the following story.

A director of older adult ministries in a local church shared her great concern for "the church's dealings with seniors." She said that the older adult ministries committee sponsored periodic church-based events that were relatively successful. They had an annual senior day and monthly daytime Bible study at the church.

The director said that it wasn't hard to generate interested leaders to organize, promote, and coordinate these events. Moreover, for a while, it wasn't hard to tap the same individual members who, in addition to her, would act independently to telephone and visit the homebound. But these individuals eventually "burned out," and the older adult ministry director admitted her discouragement that efforts did not gain wider support. She said that a lively ongoing and coordinated effort that responded to critical everyday needs of elders in and beyond the church simply didn't happen. The church had a hard time letting elders know in a systematic way that its members really cared.

As she expressed her concern and disappointment, this church leader made an immensely insightful point. She said, "I know there are some changes we can make that could make a difference. But it seems we're long on vision and short on commitment."

This director's experience is not an isolated one. Though some churches do exhibit immense commitment, obtaining committed effort in other churches is problematic. A dominant issue is that traditional meanings and values that emphasize and support commitment no longer exert the authority they did in the past. Contemporary individualistic, competitive, and materialistic values and the increasingly complex issues people face make commitment difficult. African Americans in the younger generations admit to being "pressed down and worn out by the struggle to make a life for ourselves in this society," as one young adult put it. People perceive themselves as not having the time or the energy to act on other than their own concerns (Bellah and others, 1985; Hunter, 1990; Mead, 1970).

Quite apart from this reality, people sometimes resist committed activity not simply because of its challenge but because it is too frightening. Chronic and debilitating illness, death, and other forms of suffering are realities among elders. These realities remind us of our human vulnerability. When these realities frighten us, we may divert our attention away from the very activities that are needed to sustain the sufferers. Indeed, we may act instead on the adage "Out of sight, out of mind." By our inaction and our refusal to hear the sufferers, we also intensify their felt sense of vulnerability and suffering, and we undermine what we may learn from being with and caring for them.

In one instance, an elderly man was subtly able to point out his caregiver's unwitting inattentiveness to his suffering. She had asked him, "What's been on your mind lately?" He replied that he had been thinking about being old. When she asked him to explain further, he said that he had been thinking about the commandment that says to honor your mother and father. He then said: "I wonder if I'm worth it."

This man had felt ignored and also assaulted by the debilitating changes in his body, over which he had no control. His caregiver recognized that she had not given him the reassurance of his worth as a person because of fears about her own aging that his condition provoked. Yet because she took to heart what he had to say, she resolved to find ways of giving him the reassurance he needed. The key point here is that elders in our congregations have similar experiences, and their experiences may go unheeded because of the fears of community caregivers or other deterrents to committed action.

Defining Commitment

Commitment is an indispensable requirement of all that we do to honor elders. It is an essential part of soul. But what precisely is commitment? How do we enter into committed activity with and on behalf of elders? How important is persistence to commitment?

When we speak of commitment, we refer to intentional and determined efforts to contribute to elders' experiences of positive meaning, vitality, and dignity. Furthermore, we understand it to be our self-propelled responsibility, which, in its focus on the lives of elders, contributes to the life of the whole community (Thurman, 1987).

Commitment is not a mechanical process. It is the community's agreement to act and the community's expression of its integrity. By integrity, we mean "the courage of our convictions, the willingness to act and speak in behalf of what we know to be right" (Carter, 1996, p. 7).

Entering into Committed Activity

Commitment becomes possible when we know who we are (Thurman, 1987). This is because knowing who we are grounds us in what we intend to do in ministry with and on behalf of elders. As such, our identity helps us decide our ministry direction with integrity. We are a soul community, a community in solidarity. We acknowledge our existence as living beings, an existence that carries on from the lives of our ancestors and elders. We count the present elders' lives and concerns as our own. Our identity rests on the elders' mirroring the younger generations' road ahead and the younger generations' seeing this mirror before them.

We also have a Christian identity. As a soul community, we are Christian. And because we are Christian, the actions to which we commit ourselves must reflect this identity. We recognize this identity by our roots, described by Temba Mafico in Chapter Two, and the communal ethic to which we referred earlier in this chapter. That is, we commit ourselves to actions that continue our long cultural and biblical history as a community that honors elders. We act with commitment based on Jesus' love ethic exercised through mutual care and shared resources among elders within an extended family framework.

Moreover, as committed Christians, we acknowledge that God commends elders—all persons—to us for care. We see ourselves as responsible for ensuring that care reaches those we see regularly and those we must seek out. We act with integrity on Jesus' words, "If you have done it to one of the least of these, you have done it to me" (Matt. 25:40).

We also act with integrity on the words of the apostle Paul, "Guard what has been entrusted to you" (1 Tim. 6:20). In this latter instance, our commitment to the activity of guardian has two meanings. First, we become advocates who defend and safeguard elders' rights for respect and dignity in instances where they have lost the facility of capable and mature judgment. Second, as guardians, we become supporters and preservers of elders' roles as repositories of wisdom, resourceful contributors to the community, and the recipients of care referred to in Chapter One.

Commitment as Call

God calls us to commitment with integrity. Heeding this call means, ultimately, that we corporately and consciously place ourselves in the larger spiritual reality with God at its center. It requires a process of corporate relinquishment to God's direction. It means that we agree together that we are ultimately committed to God. It means that our whole community will need to agree to discern what God is calling us to do even in the midst of great and tragic human need or challenging issues (Thurman, 1987).

It means, too, that what we finally do, to use Stephen Carter's words, "is not merely a statement, an exercise of the faculty of speech; it is quintessentially an act, and one on which others rely" (1996, p. 33). The elders will know that we mean what we say by what we do. When we heed the call to commitment in these ways, we exemplify the quality of soul.

In his discussion of commitment, Howard Thurman (1987) cautions us, however, that heeding the call to commitment can be blinding if we make an idol of it. He points out that when we become so fierce and unswerving in our commitment to what is clearly God's call to act, we can do all kinds of violence to the elders on whom our ministry focuses.

An example of this idolatry emerged in an event designed to honor elders. A local congregation planned a dinner to be attended by all its members. Younger members made tributes to the elders. Then, because they wanted the elders themselves to participate as part of their ongoing role as contributors to church life, the leader called on an elder to read the Scripture. The elder declined by saying that her eyesight would not permit it. The leader persisted in the invitation, forcing the elder to decline several times. Finally, the leader relented and asked someone else. What the leader did not know was that the elder could not read. However well intentioned the goal, its application resulted in a troubling outcome.

What Thurman suggests is that when we enter into committed activity, we do so with great humility, yet in line with God's call. In our humility, we refrain from seeing our activity as a personal achievement into which we must dive headlong without full realization of its consequences on the lives of others (Thurman, 1987). Instead, we see the giftedness of what we are called to do, the sacredness of the persons for whom we do it, and ourselves as imperfect imitators of the One who has called us into committed service.

Persistence in Commitment

Determined activity with and on behalf of elders requires steadfastness. Even though we meet with adversity, distraction, or problematic consequences in what we attempt to do, we continue toward the high-mark calling that is in Christ Jesus. When we engage in committed action with integrity, we willingly accept the consequences of our actions. We are unafraid to embrace significant challenge, cost, and sacrifice knowing that what is worth sacrificing, paying, and dying for is worth living for (Hunter, 1990).

Elders in one local congregation showed this kind of persistence in a situation where they were committed to develop a food pantry that would assist needy elders and younger families. They encountered many obstacles in their effort to be resourceful contributors to community life. At first, the church's governing body refused their proposal. When it finally accepted the proposal, the question of space and the source of the food arose. Members raised fears about burglary. They also raised concerns about the "stamina" of the elders to carry out the plan.

But the elders were not deterred by the difficulties they confronted. They considered the approval of their proposal confirmation that the pantry could and would become a reality. And they knew of the great need for it. In time, they received all the support they needed. The food pantry opened, and the elders' "stamina" did not fail.

Habits of the Soul Community

We enliven both our relationships with elders and our commitment to act in honoring ways by our development of Christian habits, particular behaviors we intentionally and consistently exhibit that show our identity as Christians. In the soul community, these behaviors are habits of the heart that reflect life in Christ and our regard for human existence across the life span as a gift created by God. Our community's development of these habits of the heart derive from our understanding that God's gift of life across the life span is worthy of honor.

By what habits do we honor? We will consider three interrelated habits that are key aspects of biblical faith: expressing gratitude, showing compassion, and remembering.

Expressing Gratitude

At an appreciation banquet for elders, the pastor and selected members gave a series of tributes to the oldest members of the church. They described the elders' roles and contributions to the church. They identified them as Christian mentors and models. They portrayed them as supportive and unforgettable friends. They celebrated their longevity. After each tribute, the banquet attendees responded with the words "Thank God, and thank *you*," adding the person's name.

We show gratitude for the presence of elders when we give thanks to God for them. The apostle Paul, in particular, thanked God continually for the love and faith of members of the churches whom he visited and in his writings. He wanted the members to know that God's presence and activity through Christ and the Holy Spirit were being made known in their actions in the community. He acknowledged their faith, love for one another, speech, knowledge, sharing in the gospel, and steadfastness of hope (Rom. 1:8; 1 Cor. 1:4; Eph. 1:16; Phil. 1:3; Col. 1:3; 1 Thess. 1:2).

Paul's expressions of gratitude for the whole membership of the church raises our consciousness about God's presence and activity through us that makes us Christians and builds us up as family and friends. It also raises our consciousness about our need to voice our gratitude. At the same time, his words of gratitude alert us to ways we may give thanks for God's presence and activity through the eldest among us. However, with particular regard for elders, Paul alerts us to the legacy of faith and encouragement handed down from grandparents and parents in his words to Timothy (2 Tim. 1:3–6a): "I am grateful to God—whom I worship with a clear conscience, as my ancestors did—when I remember you constantly in my prayers night and day. Recalling your tears, I long to see you so that I may be filled with joy. I am reminded of your sincere faith, a faith that lived first in your grandmother Lois and your mother

Eunice and now, I am sure, lives in you. For this reason I remind you to rekindle the gift of God that is within you. . . ."

We may call to mind contemporary churches where elders are honored through expressions of gratitude. However, we may also recognize the need for greater and more consistent effort in this regard. A coordinator of older adult ministries put it succinctly: "Our church has an annual worship celebration of seniors that is designed to honor them and thank them. But we need to show our thanks more often and in many more creative ways."

Showing Compassion

A minister told of an elderly church member who had had one leg amputated and was expecting to lose the other leg as well. She had also experienced four heart attacks within a period of six months. She spoke of her strong faith in God. But she also spoke of her struggles with feelings of loneliness, her suffering, and her fear of dying alone. One of the church members knew about this woman's situation and became a visiting friend as part of the church's lay visitation ministry. The visiting friend knew the woman needed a compassionate friend who could feel with her the trauma that brought her such deep feelings of loneliness and fear (Johnson, 1995).

Honoring elderly church members and other elders in situations of suffering requires compassion on our part. Compassion is the emotion we feel at the awareness of the hardship or tragedy in elders' lives. We are compassionate when we identify with them by suspending our frame of reference in order to enter into their experiences. Compassion allows us to share the concerns that weigh on them or that affect their material, psychological, social, or spiritual well-being. Compassion allows us to listen, affirm, comfort, and engage in moral discourse or decision making about right or wrong in tough situations such as the one mentioned by a husband regarding his wife: "They tell me she had a stroke. She's in a coma. She'll never be the same. They want me to say it's OK to 'pull the plug.' I don't know. What should I do?" To the extent that the soul community is a compassionate community, it honors elders.

Our ability to be compassionate derives from our acceptance of God's love for all human beings, including elders. This acceptance is integrally tied to our gratitude to God for elders. Motivation also comes from our acknowledgment that as Christians, we are called to show to others the same compassion shown by Jesus (Phil. 2:12; Col. 3:12). We are to "bear one another's burdens" (Gal. 6:2).

Remembering

Describing the nature of the church, an elderly woman said, "To me, a soul community is one that helps me get in touch with my soul—my life, who I am, where I've been, and where I'm going. To me, it's a community that encourages me to remember my story, good parts and bad parts, and lets me know it's OK—even important—for me to do that. When I was young, my 'Pop-Pop' would tell about how he grew up. I remember how he'd smile when I'd say, 'Pop-Pop, you mean that really happened?' Some of the things he'd say were so funny. But other things he'd say let you know his life wasn't easy. I remember, though, every time he'd tell his story, he'd end with 'God has brought me a mighty long way. God never forsakes us. You remember that, child.' And you know what? I'll always remember it."

When we are in a conversation with elders, it will not likely be too long before they will tell us a story that begins with "I remember." In their act of remembering, they put together the experiences of their lives and seek to make sense out of their lives. Ashbrook tells us that "meaning and the making of meaning are linked to memory. Meaning depends on memory. . ." (1996, pp. 171–172). But meaning also depends on elders' having someone with whom to share their memories.

Ashbrook further suggests that without a working and shared memory, personal identity and a sense of the past, present, and future of life are called into question. In a real way, to have a story is to have a personal soul; but to share our stories is to discover our corporate soul. When we fail as a community to welcome and hear elders' stories, we negate the elders' expression of soul as well as our own and derail both the discovery and the making of meaningful history.

When we encourage and listen to the elders' stories, we affirm their need for making meaning. In many instances, we are apt to find ourselves immensely enriched by what they have to say, and they may celebrate by reliving joyous life experiences. In other instances, we may discover deep wounds that cry out for healing. The elders' remembering evokes our own remembering. Our welcoming responses create an affirming space for our sharing stories together. We become partners in discovering what our past has to say about our present and our future.

IT IS IMPORTANT FOR ELDERS TO REMEMBER. Our recognition of the importance of remembering is fundamental to our formation of ministry with elders and on their behalf. We honor elders through an environment that encourages and invites them to remember. However, elders do not always have opportunities to tell their stories or an audience to listen to them. The routines of contemporary churches, the perceived lack of time needed for sharing stories, and the generation gap mentioned earlier undermine the ability of churches to pursue this activity. This reality should serve to remind us of our need for reflection, action, and ultimate enrichment.

IT IS IMPORTANT FOR THE SOUL COMMUNITY TO REMEMBER. We function as a caring community when we take the time to remember the elders. In interviews about how the church might best honor them, elders said time and again that they wanted to be remembered. In the words of an elderly man, "The biggest tribute, the best way that the church can honor its senior citizens, is not to forget them." An elderly woman said, "As for my church, I would not expect a lot during my times of difficulty. I would just want people to remember me with calls and cards and visits if they could." Another elderly woman said, "I think the church would encourage senior citizens by remembering and recognizing them."

We may think of the church's act of remembering in at least four ways. One act of remembering entails our making a special point of knowing who the elders are, where they are, and what their situation, needs, joys, fears, concerns, contributions to the community, and hopes are. This act is basic to all we do with them and on their behalf.

The church's second act of remembering entails our recall of those who have died. Through this recall, we show with gratitude and affection our linkage with the "cloud of witnesses" who helped create pathways on which we now walk. Such remembering reminds us of the unfolding process of life. It invites us to reflect on the things that matter to us and the direction of our communal and individual lives.

Through experiences of worship, our whole intergenerational community recognizes ourselves as a collective body and the One who calls us to be in solidarity. This third experience of communal remembering unites people at all ages and stages and reminds us all of who we are in Christ Jesus.

Finally, as a remembering community, we see the importance of the extension of the act of remembering beyond the confines of our church's physical environment. We extend it to wherever we come in contact or seek contact with elders. And we see the value of our encouraging it in its numerous creative forms such as singing, writing, and performing and visual arts.

THE BIBLE SUPPORTS REMEMBERING. A number of images of what it means to remember appear in the Bible. These images both support our development of a habit of remembering and guide us in new ways of making remembering come alive in our community.

The inclusion of genealogies in the Bible reminds us that elders, both living and departed, create our heritage and the human foundation for our lives. Our elders are the ones from whom successive generations have come (Ruth 4:18–22; 1 Chron. 2:1–15; Matt. 1:1–17; Luke 3:23–38).

The apostle Paul presents an image of arousing remembering in his Second Letter to Timothy. In the letter, Paul calls forth Timothy's mindfulness of the origin of his faith, traced to his grandmother and mother (2 Tim. 1:5). Paul seeks to arouse Timothy's recall of his elders to inspire and encourage him in his faith action. Simeon Peter also reminded early Christians of the significance of remembering the heritage on which their faith was based as means of seeing God's promise for the future (2 Pet. 3:1–4). These images of Paul and Simeon Peter alert us to the importance of stimulating the experience of remembering elders and ancestors to the end that we are nurtured by the faith handed on by them.

In his First Letter to the church of the Thessalonians, Paul tells of his own, Silvanus's, and Timothy's remembering the work of the members (1 Thess. 1:3). His words provide an image of intentionality in remembering the church's story that includes the work of all its members. Paul also charged the church at Ephesus to remember Jesus Christ as the center of their lives through whom they experience peace and oneness in community (Eph. 2:11–22). In sum, the references in Scripture present ideas that guide our development of remembering as an admirable habit and an important process for honoring the elders in the community.

Concluding Commentary

In this chapter, we have explored the nature of the soul community. In our exploration, we have learned that soul has its origins in Scripture. We learned that the soul community honors elders through specific soul relationships, including family and friends, and that these relationships have shown continuity and salience in people's lives over time. We learned that commitment is central to our establishment of soul relationships. We also discovered that an honor-bestowing community develops particular habits that are consistent with the gospel, including the habits of expressing gratitude, showing compassion, and remembering.

Questions for Reflection

1. Consider how your church responds to elders. What efforts do you favor and what efforts do you oppose? Why?

2. What words or statements would you use to describe types of relationships you have observed between younger members and elders in your church? What types of relationships you would like to see? Why?

3. Based on what you have read in this chapter, what proposal would you make that might enhance the development of soul relationships in your church? What might be the strong and weak points of your proposal? Why?

4. In what ways does your church show commitment to ministry with and on behalf of elders and to building relationships with them?

5. In what ways does your church honor elders by expressing gratitude, showing compassion, and encouraging remembering? In what ways might your church give additional expression to these habits?

4

CREATING AN
HONOR-BESTOWING
ELDER MINISTRY

Anne Streaty Wimberly

JANICE GRESHAM TELLS the following story: "When my pastor, Dr. William Flippin, at the Greater Piney Grove Baptist Church (known as 'the Grove') in Atlanta asked me to coordinate the senior ministry of the rapidly growing congregation of more than 3,500, I felt that the mission was ordained by God. I was prepared for it by many years in aging services in the public sector. I had also been involved in activities pertaining to seniors in the church. I was happy to accept the invitation. And I looked forward to what I knew was an important and necessary venture, not just because I knew I was called to do it but also because the Bible holds us responsible for honoring our elders.

"The senior ministry had actually already begun when I became the senior service coordinator. The Busy Bees were organized in 1991. This group had been the single focus and effort to involve the senior members of the church. They had joined a local organization called Reaching Out to Senior Adults (ROSA), which was designed to meet elders' spiritual needs and improve their quality of life. The seniors were also involved in various community and church projects.

"Although the senior ministry was not at first a coordinated effort, it had started as the result of a vision of the pastor resulting from his concern that men were not participating. His charge had been to organize what he called the Senior Day Out. The purpose was to bring church members, especially men, over the age of fifty-five to the church each Wednesday, with the intent of providing organized activities from 9:30 A.M. to 2:00 P.M., structured with an already functioning noonday midweek Bible study as the focal point. The program was designed around the theme 'Living the Abundant Life After Fifty-Five.' It is still going. The program consists of spiritual and informational food for thought and stewardship of our 'bodily temples' through fun, fellowship, fitness, and creative expression.

"When I came on board, my thoughts and my heart focused on the stories of elders I knew. Among those who came to mind was one of the Grove's elders we call Granny. She and I have been prayer partners. I remember her saying to me, 'Granny is not able to get around, but I'm happy.' My first task as Granny's prayer partner was to write her obituary (she organized her funeral to the last detail). To care for Granny, I also took on life sustenance tasks, such as making sure she got the benefits for which she was eligible. She always offered to pay me for my help. But I insisted that she was teaching me how to 'walk this spiritual journey.' Granny reminds me of other seniors who were referred to formal help through the senior ministry. Our seniors are so important to us, and we know it is their needs on which our ministry must center.

"With the help of a steering committee, we've been able to take the church's budding ministry a step further. Our hope was that we would become gatekeepers and quality care reviewers for the elders. The committee voiced strong opinions about the need to minister to homebound members. We sometimes forget these members, not intentionally but through oversight—'out of sight, out of mind.' We recognized that we needed reminding that they were deserving of our attention. Younger members in the various ministries of the church joined together, and teams of at least two members each were assigned to this homebound ministry. A very simple information sheet was designed, called the Home Visit Guide. We have since developed a telephone ministry, in tandem with the formal agency, Reaching Out to Senior Adults.

"The church collaborated with the Aging Network and the American Association of Retired Persons (AARP) Connections Project for their expertise in providing monthly training to prepare for our outreach efforts. We also established an AARP chapter at the church. We solicited the help of the High Museum of Art, Kroger supermarkets' senior advocate pharmacist, and local hospital staff to help us carry on additional activities. And we've advertised through the church's monthly newsletter for professionals and other interested persons within our membership to share their talents. One of the respondents to this ad was a physical therapist who volunteers an hour each week. We have also designed simple forms to document our progress and to help us consider how we can enhance the quality of our efforts" (Janice Gresham, personal communication, 1996).

_____ o _____

Church ministry with and on behalf of elders is about action. It includes the elder-focused actions of members of the church as family and friends. It includes the actions of elders by virtue of their participation as repositories of wisdom, resourceful contributors to community life, and recipients of care. It is action generated by the values we hold dear.

In this ministry, we maintain honoring the elders as an undergirding value. But in ministry, we also translate this value into a clearly planned process. We intentionally carry out honor-bestowing activities. In ministry, we also hold as nonnegotiable the value we attach to soul community because it points to our distinctive African American identity as a community of solidarity responding to individuals' needs. But in ministry, we translate it with all deliberateness into carefully planned responses that promote and assure the honor of elders. Honoring elders and acting as a soul community are both the values and the processes that undergird older adult ministry programming.

Preparing for and entering this ministry requires intentional activity. A necessary part of it is our arriving at an initial overall view of the kinds of ministry endeavors that are needed in our particular church contexts. Models of ministry help us arrive at this overall view. They tell us the kind of readiness we need to begin our process of ministry. They identify aims and the associated areas of concern and propose responses or approaches to those aims that we might emphasize in our practice of ministry. In what they reveal, models give us a guide for action. This chapter is designed to provide one such model.

We recognize that entering into coordinated older adult ministry efforts is not always easy and that resistance does occur. For this reason, we will also propose a way of addressing the model in such instances.

Readiness for Ministry

It is perhaps a cliché but nonetheless true that we must be ready to enter into older adult ministry, like any other ministry, if we are to be effective. An important way we take seriously our need for a state of readiness is by exploring answers to key questions such as these: How do we articulate our reasons for engaging in ministry with and on behalf of elders? What is the context within which such ministry is to happen? What key internal and external factors influence what we choose to do in this ministry? What is the relationship of older adult ministry to other ministries of the church?

We will give brief attention to each of these questions.

Ministry Rationale

There are many valid reasons we might give for entering into ministry with and on behalf of older adults. A rationale for this ministry is likely to be multidimensional.

EXISTENTIALLY ORIENTED RATIONALE. We may say, for example, that the perceived needs of elders demand it or that the need for ministry lies in the issues elder members and their families face every day. We may also say that the growing number of elders in our churches or the need for addressing generational conflict necessitates our programming efforts. These reasons for entering into older adult ministry are existential. They have their origin in current events in the lives of elders and the church that prompt action. We see this dimension illustrated in Janice Gresham's description of the Senior Day Out and her care of Granny.

ENTITLEMENT-ORIENTED RATIONALE. Another reason we may give for this ministry is the entitlement of elders to it. In Chapter Two, Temba Mafico reminded us that elders are due honor, respect, care, and deferential treatment by virtue of their advanced years, their wisdom, and their contributions to the community. When we choose this entitlement-oriented rationale, we assume that there is to be a strong coordinated responsibility on our part for ministry that honors them. The story at the beginning of this chapter refers to this kind of rationale in the decision of the steering committee to extend the church's ministry to homebound elders.

CULTURALLY AND BIBLICALLY ORIENTED RATIONALE. In what has gone before, we have paid attention to the cultural and biblical mandates for honoring elders for the sake of the elders and the sake of the community. We have a cultural history of honoring elders as an essential part of our peoplehood. Moreover, the Bible mandates our respect for elders as evidence of our love for God and others and to assure our own longevity. When we give these mandates as our rationale, our concern is for continuing this heritage because it is expected of us and has enriching consequences for the elders' lives in the community as well as our own. The opening story reflects this rationale in what Gresham said about her agreement to accept the position of senior ministry coordinator.

VOCATION-ORIENTED RATIONALE. When our interest in older adult ministry comes from a vision of Christian life and our recognized call by God to care for elders' needs and contributions, we describe a vocation-oriented rationale. Our vision is of relating to elders, as to others, as Jesus would relate to them, with love. And the call refers to our feelings of being summoned to do so out of our love for him.

At the center of the vocation-oriented rationale, then, is the belief that we serve elders out of our passionate love of Jesus Christ, and we derive our sense of direction from him. This rationale also centers on the call to vocation as both individual and corporate. By virtue of our identity as Christians, we as individuals and the whole church are called to service with and on behalf of elders. As a community of solidarity—a soul community—all are called to shared responsibility.

This rationale also has a volitional aspect to it. That is, implicit in it is our choosing to respond to the vision and call. As noted in Chapter Three, we are prepared to enter into committed, purposeful, and determined activity on the basis of what we know to be God's intention for life in community. And we take seriously our expression of Christian habits that reflect the nature of Jesus Christ in what we do in older adult ministry. We find evidence of the vocation-oriented rationale in references in the opening story to the coordinator's identification of her call and the pastor's vision.

We are helped by knowing that each of the rationales mentioned is valid. However, it is important that at some point we arrive at the vocation-oriented rationale. This is because it goes to the heart of who we are and our deepest motivation as a Christian community.

Contexts for Ministry

African American elders exist in a variety of family, community, and church contexts. Some spend a significant portion of their years after age sixty-five as married couples; others are single and never married, divorced, or widowed. We also find elders in both metropolitan and rural areas. They live alone, with a spouse, with family members, or in extended families. They reside in a variety of housing structures: their own homes, rented apartments, government housing, retirement communities, senior high-rises. They also live in single-room-occupancy hotels, trailer parks, shelters for homeless people, and long-stay institutions such as personal care homes, mental hospitals, and prisons. Elders also belong to churches of various sizes with varying proportions of elders.

In doing its ministry, the church as a soul community recognizes the variety of contexts in which elders live. Because this community regards all members, including the eldest, as family or friends, they seek to respond to elders' needs wherever those elders may be. This means that the community takes care that ministry initiatives within the soul community's physical location respond to the needs and expressed desires of elders from various living contexts. And we extend our ministry outside the physical bounds of the soul community in order to respond to the needs and expressed desires of elders where they are. This form of "inreach" and "outreach" ministry ensures the communal experience, the solidarity, that reflects the image of God's family and Christ's sustaining presence in the world (Evans, 1992).

Key Factors in Deciding Ministry Actions

In his congregational model of older adult ministry, James Seeber (1995) identifies two key factors that influence the development of programming: the congregation's internal and external environments.

INTERNAL ENVIRONMENT. The internal environment is a church's understanding of its identity, its leadership, the perceived need of the ministry, and the monetary and structural means needed to implement it (Seeber, 1995). Because of the centrality of honor and soul community to older adult ministry, part of the preparation associated with the internal environment needs to focus on the congregation's exploration of what these two values mean to it and how they are or need to be expressed.

Moreover, for a church to plan effectively for older adult ministry, there must be some discussion of the extent of clergy interest. The clergy's attitude toward and leadership or support of this ministry can make a difference in the church's ministry response. Clergy influence this ministry positively when they know the situations and problems of the members through constant contact with them and seek to serve as agents of the promises of the Christian story. But more than this, they become visionary leaders in ministry when they see what must be done, recognize what is at stake if it is not done, and advocate for the fullest expression of the Christian story (Foster, 1989). On this basis, clergy are also more likely to advocate for programming that meets the circumstances in which the members find themselves.

Congregations themselves will also need to explore their perceived need for older adult ministry and determine who the leaders of the ministry will be. In many instances, the ministry commences through the efforts of an individual or a self-appointed committee motivated by one or more of the rationales mentioned earlier. In other instances, leadership is recruited, as in the case of the opening story, so as to assure a coordinated effort. In all cases, however, the rationale and other aspects of the model need to be discussed in congregational meetings or designated committee meetings.

Preparation for ministry with and on behalf of elders takes place as congregations not only become convinced of the need for it but also are able to mobilize financial and voluntary support for it. Assuring financial means may require reallocating already available resources or seeking special funding through congregational appeals and grants. Voluntary support may be obtained from within the congregation as well as through collaboration with community agencies, as in the opening story.

EXTERNAL ENVIRONMENT. The external environment refers to the demographic characteristics of the elders for whom our ministry is directed. It also includes the denominational and interdenominational communities with which a church affiliates (Seeber, 1995).

We have already remarked about the variety of contexts in which elders live. As mentioned, preparation for older adult ministry necessitates awareness of these contexts and the circumstances of elders living in them. We need to be aware of the diversity of elders' interests, attitudes, abilities, income, health, and education. It may be helpful to explore these matters and their potential effects on ministry programming according to both the differing contexts in which elder members live and their various states of physical health (Seeber, 1995).

Denominational emphases on older adult ministry can have a supportive effect on what happens in our congregations. Moreover, expertise or leadership at the denominational level may assist congregations in formulating programs. Particularly in the case of small congregations, interdenominational collaboratives may be formed within geographical regions to assure needed ministry. By making connections at the denominational and interdenominational levels, we expand the boundaries of the soul community in useful and creative ways. We create a sense of solidarity that broadens the local church structures through which we carry out older adult ministry.

Older Adult Ministry and Other Church Ministries

A key challenge to African American churches is our ability to instill a sense of peoplehood that embraces people at every age and stage even though each group may be struggling in unique ways. For example, we have seen the influence of the church in the lives of youth diminish and the formation of strategies to counter this trend through new emphases on ministry with them (Foster and Shockley, 1990; Copeland, 1995). Churches want a model that "emphasizes the supportive framework of the entire community, a 'kinship network'" (Myers, 1991, p. 110).

We are seeing an emphasis on ministry with African American singles (Patterson, 1991). The return of middle-class young adults to the ecclesial flock is requiring intentional ministry to meet their needs. Lincoln and Mamiya (1990) also warn us about the urgent need of churches to respond with imagination and interest to the fractures of life experienced by the poor and other segments of the community. The unique concerns of elders add to this framework of seemingly disparate needs and competing interests. How does the church we call the soul community respond with integrity to all?

No one can deny the importance of the various responses churches must make to the concerns confronting them today. The critical issue is whether churches take seriously their responsibility to minister to all and to envision how to balance these ministries. In *African American Church Growth*, Carlyle Stewart (1994) asserts that "programs must be developed for people of all ages and categories, to meet a variety of human needs" (p. 131). Every ministry is important. He adds that we must include all the people within the communal circle because that is where a sense of belonging is created. "Through the experience of community with others—sharing life stories and collectively claiming the truths of the faith—personal and communal transformation can be realized within the context of the fellowship community" (p. 133).

Stewart rightfully frames the task of churches in a way that authenticates the inclusion of older adult ministry as an essential part of our endeavors. Moreover, in our efforts to include this ministry, we must understand that a denial of this ministry denies the church its identity as a caring and healing place. It denies the community's bond with the individuals who connect us with our past and the road ahead. It denies us the occasion for living the gospel fully.

Ministry Aims

The aims we choose for ministry with and on behalf of elders emphasize the basic valuing aspect of its development. Aims reflect what we most want to happen as a result of our ministry endeavors. They are the outcomes we deem important for elders and for the whole community. They are the basis for the actual "doing" part of the ministry.

In more specific detail, the aims for older adult ministry propose communal undertakings and life qualities that promote the elders' experiences of honor, dignity, and worth within the community. They reflect the value of honoring elders and are guided by actions reflecting these values. They also reflect the qualities we understand as indicative of the soul community, and they are undergirded by our belief that to honor elders is to cherish and care for all within the community (Gilmore, 1992).

Two aims will be considered here, along with several areas of concern associated with them. The first primary aim is the soul community's ongoing affirming response to elders' roles as receivers of care and active participants in community life. The second chief goal is to contribute to the well-being of elders in accordance with the various aspects that shape their lives.

Responding to Elders' Roles

We have stressed the role of elders as receivers of care and active participants in community life. We have identified these roles in more specific terms as recipients of care, repositories of wisdom, and resourceful participants in the community. Our aim is to affirm these roles and to respond to elders, respectfully, on the basis of our understanding of these roles.

Elders themselves give us guidance about the nature of the care recipient role and our response to them. "The church should come to the rescue when the elderly are in need," said one elder, expressing a common view. "Someone to look after us when we need it can make a big difference in our lives. Now mind you, as long as I am able, I want to do what I can for myself. Personally, my circumstances are such that I do not need for the church or my family to do anything special for me at this time. I am living just fine. I am able to care for myself. I do not want them to do anything for me I can do for myself. But there might come a time when things change." We honor elders by our validation of these roles. And we state our intentionality to do so by making clear the aim of responding affirmatively to these roles.

A reminder to us about the nature of the repository-of-wisdom role is also found in an elder's words: "I want to be able to contribute something of what I've learned throughout this life of mine. As a senior in the church, I would like the church to regard me as useful. I would also like it to provide and support ways for me to remain active and involved as long as I am able."

Elders themselves want the church to make use of their resourcefulness as community participants. They expect the church to use their leadership in church life and their knowledge about the needs of others to guide church responses. For example, as one elder said, "Everybody's situation isn't the same as mine. You know, there's folks right here in the high-rise who don't get support from family or church. They have a hard time getting the things they need. They can't get out to do what they'd like. I do what I can for them. But they really need more. Seems like somebody could do something to make life a little better for them."

Contributing to the Well-Being of Elders

The second chief and related aim is to contribute to the well-being of elders. Well-being is defined as the elders' experience of care, sustenance, and positive life meaning to which the initiatives of others and the elders themselves contribute to the extent possible.

This aim encompasses the church's intent to address several interrelated aspects, including elders' social, psychological, physical, economic, and spiritual well-being. Though each of these aspects of well-being has separate meaning, each does not stand alone. All aspects of well-being are interrelated. A deficiency in one affects an elder's experience of another. Consequently, when elders experience a sense of well-being in all aspects, they feel a sense of wholeness, a sense that the whole self is supported and nurtured (Rakowski, 1987; Moberg, 1990; Wimberly, 1994a; Ellor and Bracki, 1995; Levin and Tobin, 1995).

One elder described it as a sense of peace and worthwhileness in life. She said, "Really, I'm at peace with myself, with everything and everybody around me. By and large, life has been good. Yes, there have been struggles. There still are. But I've made it this far, thank God, and I'm going to make it on in."

She continued, "I've always said, 'There's nothing that can happen to me that God and I can't handle together.' I'm old now, you know, and I have some aches and pains. But God is good. God always sends me what I need and somebody along the way to help me out. My family and my church have been good to me. They've been right here with me all along, doing things, helping me. They let me know they're there if I need them. And they let me know they need me, too. You know, I'm on the Mothers' Board. I'm grateful. It makes my life worthwhile."

How do we understand the various aspects of well-being as aims? We may state them as follows:

• *The aim of older adult ministry is to care for elders' social well-being.* This aim focuses on the soul community's intent to promote elders' positive connectedness with their past and other people. It also highlights efforts that contribute to elders' experience of dignity and comfort in their living environment.

• *The aim of older adult ministry is to care for elders' psychological well-being.* This aim pertains to the soul community's intent to engage in guiding, sustaining, and enabling activities that contribute to elders' experiences of the self as a valued creation of God. It includes activities that contribute to their ability to deal constructively with life's changes and losses and arrive at positive life meaning.

• *The aim of older adult ministry is to care for elders' physical selves.* This aim focuses on the soul community's intent to show concern for and promote elders' bodily health. Moreover, it centers on the community's intent to give caring responses to elders and their family members during times of illness, disability, and wrestling with life-and-death dilemmas.

• *The aim of older adult ministry is to care for the elders' economic well-being.* This aim involves community attention directed toward ensuring elders of economic sufficiency and, at minimum, the basic supplies they need for everyday living.

• *The aim of older adult ministry is to care for elders' spiritual well-being.* This aim focuses on the soul community's intent to maintain opportunities for worship, study, play, and service wherein elders affirm and deepen their relationship with God, self, others, and all things and maintain a sense of life purpose.

Ministry Responses

Aims should not serve as mere formulations of intentions; they are designed to give direction to our actual "doing" ministry, what we refer in Part Two as the *practice* of older adult ministry in the soul community. We choose particular responses or approaches that help us accomplish our aims. In our choices, we also maintain awareness of the various dimensions associated with our readiness for engaging in older adult ministry. In preparation for Part Two, we will identify several ministry emphases that respond to the aims just discussed and connect ministry practices with honor as an activity.

• *Emphasize a life cycle approach to honoring elders.* Honoring elders is a life cycle undertaking. Through this undertaking, the soul community recognizes the implications of people's life cycles for the elders' and others' well-being. It directs attention toward the life cycles of individuals, marriages, and families and the role of elders in all of these. We help members become aware of how honoring elders changes according to the progression of our life cycles and what it entails within each life cycle stage. We also guide members to envision and practice ways to act on these understandings. Through this emphasis, we seek to respond to our aim to address the social and psychological aspects of elders' lives.

• *Emphasize a cross-generational approach to honoring elders.* Through this undertaking, the soul community directs attention to the significance of cross-generational connections. Through this attention, we help persons develop skills that increase positive communication, valuing, and understanding between elders and younger generations. We also create a pathway for persons to hear and respond to the needs of elders. Through this emphasis, we also act on our aim to address sociopsychological aspects of elders' lives.

- *Emphasize a contextual approach to honoring elders.* Through this undertaking, the soul community directs attention to the range of psychosocial, physical, economic, and spiritual needs of elders in the particular contexts in which they live. We identify forms of helping actions and guide the development and use of skills to accomplish these actions.

- *Emphasize a collaborative church and community approach to honoring elders.* Through this undertaking, the soul community recognizes that responding fully to the range of psychosocial, physical, economic, and spiritual needs of elders requires collaboration with agencies beyond us. As part of this undertaking, we build a viable church and community helpers' network. We provide pastoral care and nurturing. We offer programs that deal with wellness, illness, and death and ensure an environment wherein elders and family members may work through ethical dilemmas associated with life and death.

- *Emphasize a participatory approach to honoring elders.* Through this undertaking, the soul community takes seriously the notion that honoring elders and cherishing and caring for the community happens, in great measure, by "people action." Pivotal to this undertaking is our intentional involvement of elders in planning teams and initiatives designed to make a difference in their lives.

From Resistance to Action

Acting on a model of ministry with and on behalf of elders is not always easy. Indeed, it is helpful for us to be aware that resistance may be a significant factor in carrying out a ministry model. Consequently, it is important for the pastor and others who assume responsibility for this ministry to have prior awareness of the potential for resistance, be sensitive to signs of resistance, and develop skills for addressing it.

Resistance commonly takes three interrelated forms: attitudinal, interactional, and contextual.

Attitudinal Resistance

Early in this chapter, we became acquainted with a sixty-five-year-old elder who had begun to feel pushed aside. His experience is not unusual in church situations where new generations of high school and college graduates become welcomed participants in the church's ministry. In situations of this kind, a predominant attitude about the merits of "book learning" versus the elders' "living library" precludes the fullest participation of elders as resources in the soul community's life. Conversely, some elders may have internalized the attitude that they are obliged to "step aside" and to "retire" as they have done from secular work in order to make room for the young.

In these situations, the role of the pastor and older adult ministry leaders is to work toward shifting the attitudinal frame of reference away from participation based on educational and secular worklife criteria to a frame of reference that emphasizes the gospel view of all Christians as disciples and stewards in the ministry of Jesus Christ. It is necessary to communicate on an ongoing basis that all who are believers in Jesus Christ are his disciples. As disciples, all Christians are to be learners and imitators of Jesus in how they live and relate (John 8:31, 15:8; Eph. 5:1–2). Thus as Christians, the young and the old are considered lifelong learners.

As stewards, all Christians are to be guardians of God's mysteries (1 Cor. 4:1; Gal. 4:2; 1 Pet. 4:10). They are to be guardians and supporters of the faith. This also means that all Christians are to exercise stewardship by giving time, talents, possessions, and self in serving God for the upbuilding of God's household (Eph. 3:1–10; 1 Thess. 5:11). At the same time, helping members shift to a new frame of reference necessitates that pastors and older adult ministry also stress that Christians have a parallel mandate to honor elders and the gift of wisdom born of experience that they bring to the community. Because of this parallel mandate, the soul community is obliged to seek out their wisdom and leadership, to hear from them how best they may share it in the community, and to have opportunities for that to happen.

Interactional Resistance

We also learned earlier about the importance of cross-generational contact with elders in the community. Yet attempts to accomplish it can encounter resistance. People sometimes resist interacting with elders confined to home or in institutional contexts.

As a volunteer at a nursing home, I became acutely aware of the infrequency with which church members came to interact with elders both in the activities department and in the elders' living spaces. Many of the residents were well advanced in years and had few or no visits from relatives. I became acutely aware of the resistance people have to interacting with elders in this circumstance and with homebound elders.

I have since learned from my students that part of the resistance stems from the painful reminder of the changes that occur as one ages and of life's finitude. It is not easy for us to confront what may lie ahead of us or to contemplate our own movement toward death. Our way of handling our pain, our fear, our need to hold on to life as we would like it always to be sometimes causes us to resist interacting with individuals in life's final stages.

Another kind of interactional resistance occurs in our churches when generations are consistently separated during worship and Christian education. Resistance occurs when a church insists that only an age or stage approach to worship and Christian education is acceptable and when the voices of those desiring cross-generational interaction go unheeded. An elder spoke for herself and others like her: "I suppose when I had my babies in my arms in church years ago, I became a little concerned when they cried. I'm sure I took them out for a spell on more than one occasion. But still, there was no question but that they belonged with me there. I miss the sounds of children in my church now. You know, to me, the sounds of children are the sounds of life. That makes me say many times now, I get the feeling that worship is no longer alive. It really isn't. To me it seems dead."

Addressing interactional resistance requires that the soul community engage in dialogue to uncover the sources of resistance. In this sense, dealing with interactional resistance also entails dealing with attitudes and feelings. A context of dialogue is also needed in order to hear the voices of persons who suffer and grieve because of isolation brought on by minimal or nonexistent interaction. In addition, dialogue is needed to explore a range of options for addressing elders' experiences of isolation and the impact that deficits in cross-generational interaction have on the community.

Contextual Resistance

A recurring remark of elders is that church activities in which they have an interest take place at locations and times that make it virtually impossible for them to participate. Elders complain that scheduling events at the church or elsewhere at night precludes their attendance because of safety issues. Moreover, they complain that even when churches seek to make events community-accessible, they live too far away to attend. And in the case of the homebound, little thought is given to bringing events to them.

These criticisms speak to contextual difficulties. These difficulties become contextual resistance when churches fail to move beyond them. The sense of isolation that elders experience results in interactional difficulties. And the perception by churches that changes cannot be made creates an attitudinal problem. However, churches can begin to address this resistance by inviting elders' feedback on activities designed for them and the places where these are held. Churches can also begin to address contextual resistance by envisioning with elders and trying out a whole continuum of locations, activities, and times for them. The intent is to ensure elders' fullest possible participation in the life of the soul community.

Concluding Commentary

This chapter proposed a model for older adult ministry. From this model, we learned that readiness is essential. We demonstrate our readiness by formulating a rationale for our ministry, recognizing the contexts in which ministry should occur, and noting key internal and external factors that inform our ministry actions. We also demonstrate our readiness for older adult ministry by addressing the relationship of this ministry to other ministries of the church. The principal goal of this ministry is the well-being of elders, with the understanding that the well-being of elders and the well-being of the soul community are interconnected. We discovered that the "three R's" of honoring elders are integral parts of the ministry model in that elders are to be both care receivers and active contributors in ministry centered on their well-being.

We discovered that ministry that honors elders is multidirectional. An honor-bestowing ministry emphasizes honoring as an undertaking that extends across life cycles, generations, and locations. We also learned that ministry focused on elders encompasses activities of the soul community on behalf of elders as well as activities carried out with and by elders. Finally, we explored the sources of resistance to implementing a viable ministry model focused on elders and how to address such resistance.

Questions for Reflection

1. What is the nature of your church's older adult ministry? How is it now being carried out and by whom?

2. Who in your church is now taking or might take responsibility for developing and implementing older adult ministry responses to elders?

3. What aspects of readiness appearing in this chapter has your church already considered? Which ones need to be considered?

4. What attitudes and feelings would you have about your church's insistence on activities that promote elders' well-being? Why? What resistance have you observed or might be forthcoming with regard to your congregation's attitudes toward elders and ministry with them and on their behalf? What approaches to addressing existing or potential resistance might be helpful?

PART TWO

THE PRACTICE OF HONOR-BESTOWING MINISTRY

5

SHOWING HONOR THROUGHOUT THE LIFE CYCLE

Edward P. Wimberly

BACK IN 1984, I WOKE UP in the middle of the night with "Mark 7:7" in my mind. It was the first time something like that had ever happened to me. Excitedly, I ran to my Bible, thinking that a significant revelation from God had just occurred and I needed to grasp what this disclosure was. I turned to Mark 7:7, which reads as follows: "And in vain do they worship me, teaching as doctrines the precepts of men"—itself a quote from Isaiah 29:13.

I did not understand the meaning of these words at first. So I read the text of Mark 7:1–13. Suddenly, it became apparent to me that the text was dealing with honoring father and mother. The key verses were 10 and 11, where Jesus was saying that the religious traditions were ignoring the care of elders in favor of traditions that violated the law of God given in the Ten Commandments.

After some reading of commentaries it became very clear to me that the revelation from God was preparing me to deal with my aging parents and parents-in-law. Not long after this revelation, it was discovered that my father-in-law was dying of cancer. Following this, my own parents began to lose their ability to live independently. They ultimately moved in with my wife and me. When I had the revelation, I knew that I was to be a responsible adult child for my parents. The text of Mark 7 helped prepare me for the role I was eventually to play with my parents and parents-in-law. The text was not about children obeying their parents. Rather, it was about adult children caring for their aging parents when they were no longer able to care for themselves. Consequently, I learned that honoring parents had changing meanings as one progressed through the life cycle. As a child, honoring means obeying. However, honoring shifts to caring for parents when children become adults and when parents lose their independence.

———— o ————

Chapter 7 of the Gospel of Mark deals with adult children and aging parents. However, there are other passages that also deal with the life cycle and honoring. Exodus 20:12 and Deuteronomy 27:16 make clear that honoring parents involves the total life cycle rather than just the early parts. This means that honoring involves adult children just as much as younger offspring.

Honoring is an action to be taken by children toward their parents at different stages of the life cycle. This recognizes that children grow up and that honoring takes a different shape depending on the level of maturity of the children. This developmental view is not simply an imposition of modern life cycle theory on ancient texts. The ancient texts also acknowledge that level of maturity affects what people do (Knierin, 1981).

The dynamics of family relationships are often overlooked in our church ministries. It is as though we assume that this very real aspect of life in our congregations will take care of itself. Yet the biblical command to honor parents suggests that we must consider family dynamics in an intentional way. This is particularly important if our churches are to be soul communities that take honoring our elders seriously. As soul communities, the concern is for helping all, but especially elders, to maintain their emotional, physical, and interpersonal integrity and affirm the core value of honoring elders. We are invited, then, to look closely at what it means to honor our elders throughout the life cycle as one means of strengthening the solidarity of the soul community. We will begin by considering the meaning of honoring.

The Meaning of Honoring

We have seen that honor is a pivotal value undergirding ministry with older adults and on their behalf. We have also seen that in actual ministry, we translate this value into concrete actions. Our intent here is to expand what it means to act in honoring ways toward our parents from a life cycle orientation.

Honoring refers to expressing respect, esteem, regard, concern, affection, consideration, and appreciation (Fretheim, 1991). Honoring parents must be put into its proper theological context, however, before it can be fully understood.

Honoring Parents

Honoring parents is viewed as a response to what God has done, is doing, and will do as God's ongoing story unfolds. This means that the words of the law, as given by God (the Ten Commandments), are not abstract principles or propositions to be obeyed in and of themselves. God's law must be put in the context of the entire story of God and seen in terms of what God has just done in bringing the children of Israel out of slavery. Thus the law is a way in which God calls the children of Israel to accountability and responsibility. It is a call for an ethical response to God's saving and liberating activity. In reality, honoring parents is one way to respond to what God has done. Honoring parents, then, transcends our actual parents. It is a way of honoring and responding to God's love for us and our parents.

Honoring Parents During Childhood

Obedience to parents is the key theme for children. This reflects the fact that parents have guardianship of young children and are responsible for their nurturing and growth. This includes helping them develop healthy relationships and respect for elder kin and others.

The older a child becomes, the more responsibility the child assumes for his or her own behavior. As the child matures, parents can progressively relinquish parental control. This means that the child internalizes living principles as he or she matures, and the requirement of obedience to parents and respect for elders becomes an internal rather than an external matter. Reaching adulthood means assuming major responsibility for one's own behavior and attitudes as parental responsibility lessens.

Honoring Parents During Adulthood

Honoring parents as adults seems to be the focus of the Fifth Commandment. Fretheim (1991) says in connection with Exodus

20:12: "It has been shown ... that the commandment is directed
more toward adults than children. Perhaps especially in mind are cases
where elderly parents are misused or abused when working and/or
mental powers have significantly receded. This dimension shows that
obedience is not the center of what it means to honor" (p. 231).

Elder abuse, then, is a major concern of Exodus 20:12 and honoring parents. The welfare and well-being of elders is a major obligation of adult children toward their parents (Knierin, 1981).

The same themes are picked up in the New Testament in the
Gospel of Mark. In Mark 7, Jesus emphasizes the obligation of
adult children to honor parents. A controversy emerged over the
teaching of religious leaders that adult children had no responsibility for their aging parents once they paid their tithe to the church.
Jesus pointed out that this was the teaching of human beings and
not that of God. In this way, Jesus reminded the religious leaders
what the law required.

Honoring Parents During the Postparental Period

The postparental period is a modern phase of the family life cycle in
which children have become independent and parents take on the
nonparenting role of parents of adult children. At around the same
time, the parents may find themselves assuming increased responsibility for their own aging parents. Due in part to older childbearing,
parents in this "sandwich generation" may in fact have continuing
responsibilities for younger children at the same time as they must
care for aging parents. We will comment on the dynamics of honoring during this postparental period in the next section and explore
the matter in fuller detail in Chapter Six.

Honoring and the Contemporary Life Cycle

It is possible to put honoring parents into a life cycle perspective
based on the movement from obedience as children to adult obligations to aging parents. This means that as we develop through our
childhood years, we take full responsibility for ourselves and assume
adult roles in life. As we mature into adulthood, we leave home,
marry, and cleave to our spouse; and if we have children, we raise
them to do likewise. We recognize also that today many are electing
to remain single, and that the rate of single parenthood is increasing.
Brief attention needs to be paid to the latter.

The life cycle perspective is typically applied to the life cycle of the nuclear family, which consists of mother, father, and children. However, this perspective is also applicable to single-parent families, including those in shared living arrangements with parents or grandparents. Indeed, it is necessary for us to see the relevance of this perspective for these families because of their increasing number in our communities.

More and more young women are raising children without fathers. Many of these single mothers and their children reside with elderly parents or grandparents—often a single female—and rely on them for support. The salience of life cycle tasks does not diminish for these women. However, how they accomplish these tasks necessarily differs. Two key points may be made in this regard. First, shared living arrangements and child-rearing support reduce the opportunity for young mothers to learn independent parenting skills. This is particularly true in cases where parents or grandparents function more as parental replacements or primary caregivers than as supplements or mentors to their children (Apfel and Seitz, 1991, pp. 421–429). At the same time, the myriad responsibilities of young single mothers challenge their ability to care for themselves, their children, and their parents or grandparents (Dilworth-Anderson, 1992, pp. 30–31).

Second, shared living arrangements between young mothers and their parents or grandparents and the support these elders give do not invalidate the differentiation process of young mothers, but the process may be hampered. That is, when young mothers rely greatly on the support of their parents or grandparents, they do not develop the independent skills and level of differentiation needed for their ongoing survival. Likewise, while such arrangements and support do not invalidate the elders' experiences of emotional, physical, and interpersonal integrity, inordinate demand on elders to care for others is stressful and subverts their attention to their age-related needs and concerns.

The ability of young adults to honor their parents and the manner in which they do so under such circumstances are contingent upon the young adults' sensitivity to how the demands placed on elder kin can threaten the elders' well-being and quality of life. Such situations call for some tough evaluation and some decisions by elders about the limits of the support they can provide, especially in situations where they need more support than they can give, and for tough evaluation and decisions by young mothers, and indeed by all members

of the extended family, about their abilities, skills, flexibility, and re-
siliency in giving mutual care and in assuring honor to the elders.

Whether married or single, without children or a single parent,
young adult children must develop their own identity. This identity
includes their work role and often marriage and the role of parent.
At this time, our obligations toward our own adult lives, rather than
the welfare of our parents, become the dominant focus. However, as
our parents age and need our assistance or become unable to care
for themselves, we reenter our parents' lives in a new way. In other
words, when adult parents reach the juncture of launching their own
children, they often simultaneously or shortly thereafter arrive at a
point where they need to care for their own aging parents.

The critical task during young adulthood, however, is leaving
home. This task enables each young adult to establish an identity
apart from his or her parents. Failing to achieve this separate identity sets the stage for problems later when parents need care as they
age. Some adult children who have unresolved emotional issues with
their parents find it hard to think of ever providing care for their
parents. Or they may find the prospect threatening. All they can remember is their parents' trying to run their lives, and that is their
conception of caring and responsibility.

Readiness is a pivotal issue. When one couple became aware of
the possibility that the husband's mother might not be able to continue living independently, they took the time to listen to the
mother's desires and concerns. She was unready to give up living on
her own. The couple waited until the mother decided it was time to
make a move. They then brought her into their home.

Because of the level of care the mother needed, an almost complete
reversal of roles was required. It went more smoothly than antici-
pated for the mother because she was ready for it. The adult children
had considered themselves ready to receive the husband's mother. But
they were not fully aware of the unresolved issues related to their
own development toward adulthood and their relationship with the
mother. These issues began to surface after the parent moved in.

One of the adult children's tasks became working through the issues that surfaced while at the same time caring for the mother. This
task was to secure their adult identity apart from the parent's while
also respecting the parent's identity and responding with care to her
real needs.

Parents and children alike need to be aware that honoring does
have a hiatus period when establishing the adult self in the world is

more important than obedience or obligation. However, this is a period of preparation for the time when adult children must take up the care of aging parents. Those who have not developed a sense of self-differentiation will not be able to make the step toward assuming caregiving responsibility.

Typical Stages of the Life Cycle

The family life cycle typically goes through five stages: (1) the mating and formation stage; (2) the expansion stage, when children come into the family; (3) the contraction stage, when children begin leaving home; (4) the postparental stage; and (5) the aging-family stage. At each of these stages, honoring means something different. At each stage, there are at least three life cycles: for individual, marital, and family life. It is important to examine the meaning of honoring in each of these life cycles.

THE MATING AND FORMATION STAGE. During the mating and formation phase of the individual life cycle, prospective mates leave their parents and begin the process of becoming self-differentiated. Self-differentiation means becoming an independent self apart from others, especially parents. This task has already begun before young people leave home; however, leaving home greatly assists in the process.

We honor parents at this stage of the life cycle by leaving home and becoming self-differentiated. Ideally, parents can assist in this phase of the honoring process by launching their children and encouraging self-differentiation. For parents to cling to their children and insist that honoring means not self-differentiating can undermine the entire honoring process. The biblical expectation is that young adult children leave their fathers and mothers, and as they marry, they are to cleave only to the spouse.

Self-differentiation continues when people marry. The mating and formation phase of the family life cycle requires that each spouse begin to reevaluate his or her family of origin's expectations, values, and ways of doing things and determine which hinder the process of mating and formation and which aid it. Developing firm but flexible boundaries—lines of demarcation—between the new marital union and the families of origin of both spouses is essential for bonding to take place. The marital unit becomes primary for the life of the adult children's marriage and family life, and unnecessary interference from the families of origin must be resisted. This does not mean that there should be no contact. Rather, it is a matter of priorities.

THE EXPANSION STAGE. The expansion phase of the family life cycle involves the addition of children to the family if couples so choose. Here the principle of primary loyalty to our own created family rather than the family of origin remains central. The boundaries that separate the created family from the family of origin must remain firm. To give primary loyalty to our created family is not to dishonor our mother and father. Rather, it is a means of providing an environment for our expanded created family to grow and develop.

Here again, we honor our parents by protecting the boundaries of the family of creation. However, this protection does not exclude grandparents from the children's lives; on the contrary, including them teaches children the meaning of honoring the elders. But responsibility for the children and their rearing belongs to the parents rather than the grandparents.

Honoring parents in this context means protecting the parental responsibilities of the family of creation from disruptive intrusions from grandparents. Grandparents and their adult children must work out an arrangement whereby grandparenting becomes a way of assisting their adult children in their parenting. It is important that there be mutual understanding of the parental role while recognizing the grandparents' need for connectedness and their contributions to the relationship with grandchildren. This recognition is a part of showing honor.

Of course, intergenerational conflicts sometimes occur between adult children and their parents who have become grandparents (McGadney, Goldver-Glen, and Pinkston, 1987). These conflicts often center around the raising of grandchildren and how best to raise them in a hostile American culture. Often the conflict centers on "old-fashioned beliefs" of African American grandparents about the best way to raise children. These beliefs have to do with religious preferences and disciplinary practices.

Many elders believe that their old-fashioned values are the cornerstone of African American family stability and have difficulty accepting the way their adult children are rearing their grandchildren. Sometimes the behavior of a grandparent, particularly the grandmother, becomes troublesome when she assumes a controlling and authoritarian stance in relation to her own children and grandchildren (McGadney, Goldver-Glen, and Pinkston, 1987). In this context, the conflict between leaving and cleaving clashes directly with honoring parents. It is important in this context to recall that honoring for adult parental children means setting firm and clear boundaries for grandparents.

Another intergenerational problem exists in some African American families when adult children abdicate their role as parents, and grandparents are forced to provide the rearing for their grandchildren. When adult children abandon their responsibility, the elder often feels obligated to move in and take over. Clearly, the adult child's shirking of responsibility does not honor the grandparent. Honoring in this context means taking full responsibility for one's own family of creation and allowing the grandparent to help out along parent-determined lines. Of course, there may be times when adult children cannot meet their family obligations and grandparents volunteer to help out. Here the arrangement is temporary, and the grandparent and parent have an agreement that the parent will resume the parental role as soon as circumstances permit.

THE CONTRACTION STAGE. As young children move through the transitions of childhood to adolescence and then to young adulthood, the process of family contraction begins. We launch our children. Our role shifts to that of parents with adult children. Our parents become middle-aged adults, and our grandparents advance in the aging process. During this time, we begin to move toward our own middle-aged years. We begin to think about the welfare of our aging parents and consider our grandparents' needs for assistance.

The process of honoring shifts back toward our aging parents and, to an appreciable degree, away from our family of creation. It is ideal if the contracting family has launched the children, in which case the children have assumed responsibility for themselves. This lessens the pressure on the middle-aged adult children, and they have more energy to extend their care and concern for their aging parents.

However, if children have not been launched and the aging parents are becoming increasingly dependent on their own children, being sandwiched between the generations can be very difficult on middle-aged children. In this regard, there are instances in African American families where adult grandchildren respond to the need for care of elderly grandparents because of the inability of their parents to do so. Moreover, single unmarried adults also take on the responsibility of caring for their aging parents.

The point to remember here is that one of the major reasons for the young adult to self-differentiate and develop an independent sense of self as a means of honoring is to prepare for the postparental period when the focus shifts to increasingly dependent parents.

THE POSTPARENTAL STAGE. Typically, in the postparental stage of the life cycle, parents have launched their children and are either anticipating or actually entering the grandparent role. In this stage, we develop grandparenting skills, most often in the process of relating to our grandchildren and their parents. As indicated earlier, in some cases we as grandparents are called upon to become primary caregivers for grandchildren and even for great-grandchildren.

Optimally, the honor accorded to elders in their postparental stage takes the form of adult children's vigilance to their role as responsible adults and parents, and of their providing opportunities for nonprimary grandparent-grandchild relationships to develop. In the present time of increasing divorce rates and reconstituted families, however, honoring happens as adult children and their parents work through sensitive relationship issues that could separate them, and grandparent and grandchild.

More will be said in the next chapter about situations of primary care of grandchildren that make the optimal view of honoring difficult to achieve. At this point, however, we do need to be aware that elders in their postparental stage are not passive participants in the affairs of life. Honoring them means that they are accorded the right to decide the shape and direction of their lives.

THE AGING-FAMILY STAGE. More people are living longer. In fact, the fastest-growing group of elders comprises those eighty-five years and older. With advancing age, elders may confront varied changes in physical and mental health, economic situation, living arrangements, and relationships with others, including spouses, children, and other kin. These changes have consequences, but at the same time there are stable aspects of our lives—values and attitudes we hold, our outlook on life, and the endearing approach we take to having lived to this point and to what is yet to come.

These realities of aging exist within the context of our families, whether blood kin or extended. To the contrary, what happens to us in our aging years happens to the family and requires the attention of the family. Consequently, to speak of the aging-family stage is to be concerned with the ongoing aging processes of persons within the family and that call for caring relationships. Honoring, then, takes the form of including elders as part of family life. It includes being a willing presence and being attentive to elders' situations, collaborating with elders in addressing their concerns, and providing or locating assistance when needed.

This view of honoring does not mean that the welfare of the aged family member is the only concern of family members. While family members are committed to honoring elders in the aforementioned ways, they have concurrent life goals of their own, often including the care of others. Moreover, aging family members often have the goal of contributing to family life in whatever way they can and as long as they can. For this reason, we expand our understanding of honoring to include family dialogues in which both elders and younger family members articulate their multiple concurrent goals and seek together workable plans (Silverstone and Horowitz, 1992, pp. 29–30). We also work out together potential responses to health care and other situations to be used in the event of the elder's incapacity to decide (Mishkin, 1992).

Issues in the Life Cycle Honoring Process

As indicated earlier in this chapter, we run into difficulty when we have unresolved childhood issues with our aging parents at the same time as we are being called on to be their primary caregivers. We must be aware that aging parents may become dependent on their children to a greater or lesser extent, if they live long enough. Children who have self-differentiated are in a better position to accept the role of caregiver for a parent. Adult children who are less self-differentiated and who have unresolved conflicts or resentments from childhood will have greater emotional difficulty in assuming the caregiver role. Let us not forget that aging parents are still parents, and memories of the past die slowly. Adult children who are well differentiated can expect resurfacing problems, but they are better equipped to handle them than the less well differentiated. We will spend more time on the issue of self-differentiation in the next chapter.

Married couples can also expect added pressure on their marriages because the situation often reopens issues that may have a direct impact on the marriage. Let us revisit the couple who took on the caregiving role for the husband's mother.

The couple found themselves reliving some of their marital issues that involved both his mother and his father. The wife relived some hurtful experiences of feeling unaccepted by her husband's parents. The husband found himself slipping back into roles that he had when he was a child. And he was reminded on numerous occasions by his mother that he was just like his father in some of the ways he behaved. It became painfully clear that he was an offspring of his parents not just biologically but also in terms of certain behaviors.

These discoveries had negative and positive results. The positive side was that both husband and wife worked to come to grips with their issues. The wife recognized that her mother-in-law had long before changed to a real acceptance of her, which had been demonstrated on a number of occasions. They learned what behaviors of the husband's were hard to change and why. The negative side was fearing that he was stuck with irritating behaviors forever.

The honoring of parents by caring for them when they become dependent in old age is a biblical expectation. This preserves the social order and contributes to the welfare of all involved. Even when social security and pensions are adequate, often adult children must still assume caregiving responsibility or will be called on to assist in the decision making regarding what must be done to ensure adequate care. Even if parents need nursing home care, the role of adult children is still very important. Scripture clearly expects adult children to assume this role.

Honoring in the family life cycle means different things, depending on the stage of the life cycle. A key role of the church in this process is making people aware of the meaning of honoring at the different stages of the life cycle.

Dynamics of Honoring in Cases of Parental Abuse

We recognize that our parents are not perfect. Some parents are abusive, incompetent, irresponsible, and inept. Many try hard and fall short, but are not abusive. But as Christians, we claim God's grace and parenting expressed through God's love, salvation, liberation, and life's possibilities in spite of abuse or ineptness. And we see in our parents the human source of our own lives. Our experience of God's parenting, often known to us through other caring adults, frees us to see ourselves as other than abused and our parents as other than abusers. Though we do not accept or justify their abuse, we discover ways of honoring them in spite of it. In a sense, we may say that honoring parents under these circumstances is doing so whether we feel they deserve it or not. But in a broader sense, we show honor out of our love and appreciation of God's faithful parenthood to us and God's continued love for our parents even in their failures.

God's parenting acts form the foundation of the solidarity of relationships in the soul community. It is not by our effort alone that parents are honored. Rather, it is God's love for all within the soul community that sets in motion the honoring not only of parents but of every person. All human beings have value and deserve to be honored for their sacred worth.

Theological Considerations

Honoring parents who are abusive requires further theological qualification. Biblically and theologically, the qualification can be found in Ephesians 6:1–4: "Children, obey your parents in the Lord, for this is right. 'Honor your father and mother'—this is the first commandment with a promise—'that it may be well with you and that you may live long on the earth.' Fathers, do not provoke children to anger, but bring them up in the discipline and instruction of the Lord."

This passage indicates that parents have obligations to children, and provoking to anger presupposes some abusive behavior by parents. The passage recognizes that parental power could be corrupt and that power can be misused. "And where is the temptation to the misuse of power more insidious than in the parent-child relationship?" (Buttrick, 1953, p. 731).

This qualification helps us put parental honoring in its proper theological context. Honoring parents is put in an ideal setting where parents are in union with God through Christ. In this state, the passage assumes that parents have the best interests of the child at heart and can raise children nonexploitively and without abuse. However, outside of this state of union with Christ, abuse may occur and can provoke a child to anger.

Behavioral Considerations

I have worked with adult children whose parents abused them physically and sexually. They struggled with what it meant to honor a parent who was abusive, exploitive, and irresponsible. I have gained several insights from counseling with them. First, honoring does not mean that children should be obedient to abusive parents. Second, honoring parents does mean reporting abuse so that parents can be held accountable and offered help for their abusive behavior. There are many cases where abuse had been reported to the nonabusing parent and was ignored. Children must be encouraged to report abuse to nonabusing parents and authorities so that they can be protected. The church should not ignore abuse; nor should it fail to provide preventive training for parents and children.

Third, honoring involves adult children in particular holding parents responsible for their behavior by seeking the parents' acknowledgment of the abusive behavior and repenting from it before reconciliation can be made. Often children have to go through significant emotional therapy before they can confront a parent who behaved irresponsibly. Confrontation is a major psychological step. If the parent acknowledges the abuse and seeks help, the adult child can begin to think about the possibility of reconciliation. Reconciliation is not warranted until the parent acknowledges the abuse and takes steps to end it.

I am aware of a case where an adult child came to pastoral counseling after having earlier been sexually abused by her father. The abuse was affecting her current relations with male peers. Through therapy, she was able to confront her father about what he had done to her. The father acknowledged in the counseling setting that he had abused his daughter sexually. And he indicated that he would do whatever he needed to do to make sure he corrected the emotional damage.

The father explained that the abuse occurred before he was saved or in Christ and that he had repented and told his wife and family what he had done. He asked for his daughter's forgiveness, and she was able to forgive him eventually. She was not able to do so immediately. He had stopped the abusive behavior many years ago, and he knew eventually there would be a time of reckoning for him. When that time came, he was able to deal forthrightly with his past behavior.

In a large number of cases, confronting the abusive parent may not have positive consequences. However, that the adult child has matured to the point of being able to confront the abusive parent is a positive outcome. Such adult children are often disappointed when parents cannot respond positively to the confrontation, but they do not feel an obligation to pursue a relationship with the parent. In short, the command to honor parents does not require remaining in relationships with abusive parents.

Many adults who were abused by parents when they were children have many unresolved personal issues as adults. Even though they may have cut off relationships to stop the cycle of abuse, there comes a time when they must work through their feelings about the abusive parent for their own emotional and spiritual well-being. Holding on to past hurts can prevent adult children from experiencing deep happiness and hamper their ability to honor others.

For example, a man whose mother was extremely abusive to him both verbally and physically held on to the hurts so long that they prevented his achieving meaningful spousal relationships in a series of marriages. Unresolved issues with his mother kept him from full commitment in marriage: too often he saw glimpses of his mother in his wife, and he could not separate his relationship with his mother from his relationship with his spouse.

The Role of the Church in the Honoring Process

The church as a soul community has a vital concern with being a support system to protect the emotional, physical, and interpersonal integrity of elders. Our role as a support system is to offer our members educational opportunities that allow them to explore the meaning of honoring parents from a life cycle perspective. Our role is also to employ intervention strategies when needed.

The Educational Role

This community has an important educating role. The educational goal is to help people understand what it means to honor father and mother in order that they may act in appropriate ways. Consequently, the study and discussion of Scripture and the different expectations regarding honoring are important learning experiences to undertake within our churches. This calls for serious study of the biblical meaning of aging, including commentaries on specific passages where honoring father and mother occur in Scripture and engaging in dialogue about their meanings and importance for church and family life. Key passages include Genesis 20:12, 21:15, 17; Exodus 21:17; Deuteronomy 5:16, 27:16; Proverbs 3:9; Matthew 15:4–6, 19:19; Mark 7:10–13, 10:19; Luke 18:20; Ephesians 6:2; and 1 Timothy 5:8.

Moreover, it is important for churches as soul communities to offer opportunities for family members to explore the family life cycle processes in relationship to these biblical passages. Through these opportunities, for example, the passages that deal with adult children leaving home and the family life cycle can be studied and discussed. These passages are Genesis 2:23–25 and Ephesians 5:31.

The Intervention Role

Sometimes intervention in the lives of families is needed when serious problems arise. Families today seek guidance in parenting young children and adolescents and in responding to their various developmental needs. Helping parents understand and respond to their children's developmental needs lays the foundation for children to honor them and to relate in positive ways to older adults. As this happens, we make the soul community a true support system.

Concluding Commentary

This chapter has emphasized that honoring our elders is a life cycle undertaking. Consequently, honoring is not simply to be accorded to parents by young people. From a biblical point of view, honor is also to be shown by adult children to their aging parents. It is to be expressed in accordance with the predictable transition points in the family life cycle.

We have discovered that identity, differentiation, unresolved emotional issues, and other pressing concerns in the contemporary life cycle inform the manner in which we honor family elders. We have also learned that honoring means something different in each of the five typical stages of the life cycle. An important task of our churches is to create opportunities for families to explore the distinctive characteristics of honor related to family issues across the life cycle and the tasks of family members at each stage. When our churches include this task among their ministries, they become hospitable extended families that bespeak their "soul."

Questions for Reflection

1. Recall when you first became aware of or heard the phrase "Honor your mother and father." How old were you? Who said these words, or where did you read them? What did these words mean to you when you first heard or read them?

2. Has the meaning of "honor your parents" changed as you have grown older? In what ways has the meaning changed? In what ways has it remained the same? Describe any tensions that helped to bring about change.

3. Describe any ways in which you have honored your parents at different stages of the life cycle.

4. Read each of the biblical verses dealing with honoring parents identified in the text and also the paragraphs of Scripture surrounding it. Identify what the writer is talking about in the passage and how the verses relate to the overall context. What is the meaning of honoring for this particular text?

5. Compare the meaning of honoring derived from your family of origin with the meaning found in Scripture. Indicate the similarities and differences. Which meanings seem most helpful and relevant for you?

6

SUPPORTING CROSS-GENERATIONAL RELATIONSHIPS

Edward P. Wimberly

A FIFTY-YEAR-OLD DIRECTOR of Christian education in a local church shared her memory of life in a three-generation household and what it taught her about the care of elders and the church's responsibility for them:

"I grew up during a time when 'the family' for many black people was made up of as many as four generations all living under the same roof. My family happened to have been a three-generation household. I was the youngest of five children. I grew up in the absence of a father. My father had been killed in a truck-train accident before I was born; therefore, the parenting in my home was done by my mother and my grandmother. I was not aware of it then, but I later came to realize that growing up in an intergenerational family cluster was, for me, a blessing of inestimable worth.

"My mother and my grandmother seemed to have been the perfect complement to each other. My grandmother, who was born seven years after the emancipation of slaves in this country, was a person of strong constitution, strict discipline, high standards, and great wisdom. She claimed and was accorded without question her place at the head of the family at large. She was in every sense of the word the *matriarch*. My mom was a softer, gentler version of my grandmother. She brought to the situation the delicate balance that was needed in the parental relationship. Though she, too, was from the 'old school' and was very much a no-nonsense person, what she offered in the way of self was a sweet, kind embrace, which I welcomed and received.

"My grandmother died at the age of ninety-seven and my mother at eighty-three. During the course of their lives, I came to understand and to witness what it meant to 'grow old.' I saw in them the mystifying cycle of life return, in a sense, to the place where it began—to the point of greatest human vulnerability. I saw in my grandmother a bond that she shared with my baby daughter: she needed particular and deliberate care.

"I watched my mother and my aunt lovingly give her that care. They cared for my grandmother out of an inherent sense of loyalty and duty. In what they did, I learned how important our elders are and how necessary it is for me and every generation to have the same sense of obligation and responsibility. Herein lie strong implications for the church as it attempts to fashion a senior ministry that will sufficiently address the distinct concerns of the elderly. I believe that the church must be intentional in its efforts to avoid the tragic mishap of pushing our elders out onto the fringes of church life. As guardians of the faith, the church must hold in healthy tension the life thread that connects each generation and keep our elders central to the life of the church" (Rev. Danella P. Fogle, personal communication, 1996).

———— o ————

As indicated earlier, respect for elders is not just an ethical response that has informed the religious undergirding of African Americans. African Americans have also inherited an African legacy of respect for elders that crosses the generations. Not only has this heritage left us the importance of elders in the ongoing life of the community, but it has also given us a comprehensive view of reality that informed everything Africans did. African Americans inherited this worldview, and it is in intentionally connecting with it that makes honoring elders important. That is to say, honoring elders is an important way of connecting with an ongoing source of care and nurture that can sustain meaningful life for African Americans. Honoring elders is an important dimension that helps foster solidarity of relationships and builds the supportive dimensions in the soul community.

Honoring parents in the biblical tradition is accompanied by the promise of long life. The meaning of this promise relates to in-

creased meaning and quality of life for adult children. It is important that our churches take this reality seriously. This is particularly the case because, as indicated in Chapter One, many African
American churches are experiencing separation of the generations, and generational conflict jeopardizes the quality of life in
the community and undermines honor-bestowing relationships.
We must keep in mind, however, that the promise of life quality
and honor-bestowing relationships are better understood when
the benefits of honoring parents are explored in depth. We must
understand that honoring parents means that adult children are
brought into contact with a legacy of values that have sustained
life for generations.

One way to understand the promise of long life if parents are
honored is for us to explore what happens when a person gets cut
off from parents and extended family when they become adult. One
instance came when a single mother raising teenagers felt the need to
reestablish a relationship with her parents that was broken many
years earlier when she decided never to return home. Because of sex-
ual abuse at the hands of relatives, but not her parents, she had qui-
etly left home as a young adult, saying nothing. For years she had
only minimal contact with her parents, via the telephone and
through her children, whom she did send to visit. Her parents often
asked when she was coming to visit and if there was anything
wrong. She would be evasive and change the subject.

When her daughter was seventeen, she learned that the youngster
had been molested by the same person who molested her. That revelation convinced her that the secrets of the past must not continue.
She decided to return home to expose the culprit and to reconnect
with her parents.

When she revealed the abuse, her parents responded very positively to her, and her mother was able to tell her of abuse she had encountered in her own life. This woman's return home put an end to
a multigenerational cycle of abuse.

In this context, honoring parents means staying in touch and visiting every now and then. This woman had lost direct, personal
touch and only later realized that she felt that she was dying inside
because of it. After she restored her relationship with them, she felt
alive again. Honoring her parents by staying in touch and relating to
them brought benefits to her. Reconnecting brought added meaning
to her life and also enriched the lives around her.

Support System Values

Cross-generational relationships bring adult children back in touch with enduring and nurturing values that add to the quality of life. Andrew Billingsley in *Climbing Jacob's Ladder* (1992) has identified some of these enduring values of African Americans. They include the primacy of family, the importance of education, the necessity of hard work and personal enterprise, community-mindedness, espousal of the rights and responsibilities of freedom, and loyalty to country and democratic values (p. 72). These values are transmitted from one generation to the next, and they are soul community values that nurture and support the younger generations. Billingsley points out that African Americans continue to make connections with the values from their heritage through cross-generational connections.

Honoring elders also brings the younger generations into contact with religious and spiritual values that have undergirded African American life. Nancy Boyd-Franklin (1989) has pointed out that spiritual beliefs are part of the survival system of African Americans. This system includes core beliefs, among which are God's providence, justice, omnipotence, omniscience, goodness, and grace. The system includes as well the dominant themes of the equality and uniqueness of persons, the family of God and humanity, and perseverance (Mitchell and Lewter, 1986).

In addition, cross-generational honoring brings African Americans in touch with a legacy of family values. These values are grounded in Africa and are central in extended family life. They include cross-generational relationships, the importance of children in the extended family, accountability for children, reciprocity among family members with regard to roles for the sake of family survival, balancing the rights of individuals with the requirements of the family, and balancing one's own needs with those of the family (Billingsley, 1992). Honoring, then, keeps African Americans in touch with significant ties that sustain them.

Honoring elders incorporates structures that help African Americans survive despite the reality of racism. For example, the extended family functioned as a support system that brought a variety of benefits to the younger generation. Families provided support in life crises, validation for personal worth and identity, satisfaction of nurture and dependence needs, outlets for expressing strong feelings, opportunities to identify with common spiritual values, and religious grounding to deal with life cycle events and life situations (Wimberly, 1976).

Thus, honoring parents has many benefits, particularly for adult children. Moreover, refusing to honor parents—say, by failing to provide care when they are ailing—has the great disadvantage of cutting oneself off from a source of nurturing and sustenance, the means whereby one's emotional and spiritual integrity is sustained. One of the major drawbacks of living in the United States and being influenced by a market-oriented culture is the risk of being cut off from extended family roots. Productivity- and market-driven economies often uproot families and make it difficult for them to maintain emotional and geographic closeness with other family members, including elders. People's preoccupation in these economies is on keeping up, getting ahead, and satisfying the self's own financial needs. Of course, some families keep contact and intentionally nurture emotional ties with extended family members. But this is not true of all families. Failure to do so risks severing the very ties through which members may honor elders and receive deeper personal and communal satisfaction. Cutting oneself off from extended family roots for any reason is a way of committing slow emotional and spiritual suicide. Refusing to care for aging and dependent parents has precisely that effect, and the consequence is self-destruction.

Evidence suggests that African Americans are very aware of the benefits of maintaining cross-generational ties. Nancy Boyd-Franklin (1989) points out that middle-class African Americans maintain close ties to their extended families, even though bonds across generations have often been thought of in this community as hindrances to upward mobility. Thus there is evidence that generational boundaries among African Americans are less rigid and more open to cross-generational influences. This lends itself to knowing parents. Moreover, it fosters emotional and spiritual survival. Such openness encourages honoring parents as well as strengthening the cross-generational supports needed for survival in a hostile environment.

Behavioral Science Theory and Cross-Generational Honoring

The emergence of family systems theory has increased the possibility of augmenting a conceptual understanding of honoring parents. As indicated, honoring parents by adult children is a cross-generational occurrence that not only benefits the elders but also enriches the adult children in terms of quality of life. The conceptual theory that helps explain how cross-generational honoring works comes from family systems theory.

We will try in this section to explicate how honoring can be done by adult children in ways that increase their integrity as adults. Honoring is understood here as maintaining connections with older generations and recognizing how these connections can contribute to the well-being and life quality of both adult children and their forebears.

Individualism has been a major theme in American culture and in the psychology movement. Individualism often relates to the pursuit of one's own self-interest and autonomy at the expense of more communal and relational values. Some psychological theories have added to the problem by overemphasizing autonomy and underemphasizing connecting or relational values. However, the emergence of family systems theory has helped behavioral scientists visualize how the quest for autonomy is intricately related to cross-generational connections. More precisely, family systems theory has helped contemporary society envisage how positive cross-generational connectedness facilitates autonomy and self-differentiation. It has already been pointed out that cross-generational connectedness facilitates honoring. This section will provide behavioral science supports for honoring parents based on research and theory.

Perhaps the most influential family thinker to provide a theoretical base for understanding the significance of honoring parents is Murray Bowen. Building on his psychiatric background, Bowen has been one of the leading figures in marriage and family therapy (Nichols and Schwartz, 1991). Bowen's early formulations of family systems theory related to thinking about basic and core life forces that undergird the lives of individuals. He developed theoretical ideas linking individuals with families.

Bowen (1978) postulated that there were two core tendencies in human beings that were opposite yet not contradictory but complementary: the push for self-differentiation and the thrust toward togetherness. Both have to be expressed. Consequently, to be mature human beings, individuals have to move toward self-differentiation, or separation from one's family of origin, while simultaneously maintaining emotional connectedness and relatedness to it.

The dual life force emphases set forth by Bowen have implications for our understanding of honoring. The basic implication is that honoring involves both separation from parents as well as connectedness to them. Applying Bowen's ideas on separation and connectedness to the life cycle of human beings shows that at each stage, the balance between self-differentiation and connectedness changes. As a person matures chronologically, autonomy normally increases. Yet at the same time, the person's ability to participate in the family as an autonomous individual increases as well. The ideal, in Bowen's mind, is that an adult must be able to participate in his or her family of origin as an autonomous person who is self-differentiated. He believes that the self-differentiated person has the ability both to relate to family-of-origin members and to be apart from them.

Honoring parents involves separation from and connecting with them, depending on where one is in the life cycle. In addition, self-differentiation facilitates honoring parents. The opposite of self-differentiation is fusion or loss of one's separateness in the family of origin. Fusion means being swallowed up into the family at the expense of one's own uniqueness. Such swallowing up makes it difficult for adult children to honor parents. In fact, it may cause resentment and hostility toward parents. Consequently, the further that adult children move up the self-differentiation ladder, the better they will be able to relate to aging and dependent parents.

Bowen is also concerned with the increasing self-differentiation of people because this is so beneficial for all members of the family. His whole therapeutic approach is geared toward helping people achieve the self-differentiation goal. The cornerstone of his therapeutic approach is an attempt to help people "return home" in order to achieve self-differentiation. In other words, he does not believe that emotional or physical distancing helps in the self-differentiation process. Bowen has spent much of his clinical time helping people return home for the purposes of self-differentiation.

The methods that Bowen has developed to assist people to return home can also be used to enhance adult children in honoring their parents.

The Family Genogram

A key aid in honoring parents is the family *genogram* (see Figure 6.1). According to Nichols and Schwartz (1991, p. 392), Bowen defines genograms as "schematic diagrams of families, listing family members and their relationships to one another. Included are ages, dates of marriage, deaths, and geographical locations. Men

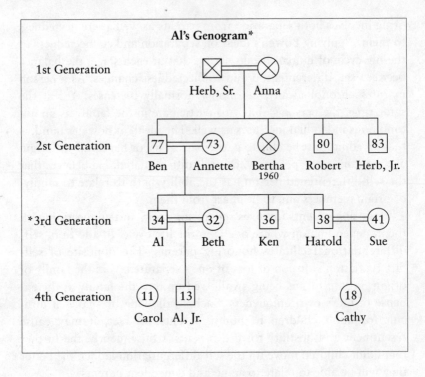

Symbols

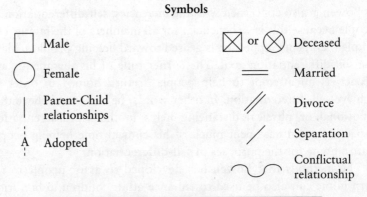

Figure 6.1. Sample Genogram.

are represented by squares and women by circles. Horizontal lines indicate marriages with dates written on the line, and vertical lines connect parents and children." The goal of the genogram is to help adult children describe family relationships rather than to make conclusions about them, to help members picture the family as a whole, and to reveal where some of the problems of self-differentiation might lie.

A genogram is a road map of the family across three or four generations. It can reveal family strengths as well as factors that led to difficulties. The goal of the genogram is to get you back in touch with your family of origin and its history, and to help you become aware of how your extended family operates and functions (Nichols and Schwartz, 1991). Using the genogram often involves returning home to collect data and information that might fill in the gaps and help in the process of awareness. Returning home to collect data from other family members initiates the honoring process in that relational contacts are being made with extended family members, and this could involve aging parents. If you are anxious about doing this but would like to do it, contact a professional marriage and family therapist as you construct your genogram, and explore its implications for your self-differentiation. Pastors and leaders of older adult and family ministries may also invite a professional to lead this process with adults in the congregation.

Significant information about cultural, ethnic, and religious connections can be derived from preparing the genogram. The following is a list of information to be gathered:

- Names, ages, and state of health
- Dates of births, deaths, marriages, divorces and separations, serious illnesses, rites of passage—leaving for college, moving to new house, and so on
- Physical location and patterns of cohesion—where significant family and extended family members live, extent of contact, and so on
- Sibling position, source of support or conflict
- Emotional cutoffs
- Education, occupation, job history
- Ethnicity and religious background

The genogram in Figure 6.1 is a sample. It is a four-generation model. The symbols used to construct the genogram appear underneath it. The adult child who constructed this genogram appears at the beginning of the third generation, followed by the spouse and siblings. The second generation level represents the adult child's parents, aunts, and uncles, and the first generation level represents the adult child's grandparents, great aunts, and great uncles. The fourth generation level represents the children of the adult child.

To complete your own genogram, list the appropriate names beneath each symbol and the ages of living relatives inside the symbol. Use the appropriate marks to indicate relatives who are deceased and those who are married. Show the dates of death and marriages if you know them. Finally, while constructing the genogram pay attention to your thoughts, feelings, body posture, and other nonverbal communication.

Making Contact with Extended Family

Bowen feels that persons should not return home to reconnect without first having some ideas about how to participate in the family-of-origin process. The danger in returning home includes the possibility of resuscitating old family patterns and reinforcing dysfunctional ones. Consequently, returning home by adult children for the purpose of self-differentiation has to be intentional. The skills and techniques recommended for the returning-home process are building person-to-person relationships with family members, controlling emotional reactivity, and extricating oneself from emotional situations (Wimberly, 1982).

BUILDING PERSON-TO-PERSON RELATIONSHIPS. Bowen feels that the core of self-differentiation is working on the core personality's need for togetherness. That is to say, working on the need to be related and connected is essential in any self-differentiation process (Bowen, 1978). Moreover, maintaining connectedness to the extended family, particularly with aging parents, also responds to the aging parents' need for connectedness to succeeding generations. Consequently, building person-to-person relationships is a prerequisite in the self-differentiation process.

Building person-to-person relationships involves choosing one extended family member at a time with whom to reconnect. It also involves the adult child's steering the conversation away from impersonal subjects and away from conversations about other family members. This step is an attempt to engage one family member in conversation about the relationship that has existed between the adult child and the family member. Sometimes, having conversations about less controversial areas of the relationship is more productive than going directly to conflict areas. Saving the conflictual conversations until later in the process is very beneficial.

Choosing one member at a time is also helpful because the adult child is more equal with one family member than with more. Two or more family members could easily overwhelm the adult child and reinforce non-self-differentiating patterns.

CONTROLLING EMOTIONAL REACTIVITY. The heart of Bowen's approach involves lessening the emotional overreaction that an adult child has to his or her family of origin. This means that self-differentiation is learning not to be anxious about being different from other family members and existing apart from family-of-origin dynamics. Bowen feels that one becomes nonanxious by lessening emotional reactivity to the family and by becoming more proactive, acting on one's self-understanding and personal values rather than reacting to external stimuli coming from the family of origin.

There are four crucial steps for reducing emotional reactivity. The first is to refuse to defend oneself to one's parents. Defending and justifying oneself to parents is reactive rather than proactive. It also keeps one locked into family dynamics and militates against self-differentiation.

The second skill in avoiding emotional overreaction is to refuse to attack or counterattack. Attacking and counterattacking are also reactions that keep the adult child in bondage to family-of-origin dynamics.

The third skill requires that the adult child avoid confronting parents about past mistakes and current problems. Confrontation often makes the parents double their efforts to keep the adult child tied to existing family patterns. In other words, confrontation reinforces enslaving family patterns.

Finally, it is important to avoid overanxious self-assertion. Nonanxious self-assertion communicates self-differentiation, but overanxious self-assertion communicates the opposite. Nonanxious self-assertion is being able to take a position on an issue and use "I" messages that communicate one's position on things. Nonanxious self-assertion enables parents to lower their defenses and become more supportive of the self-differentiation of the adult child.

EXTRICATING ONESELF FROM EMOTIONAL SITUATIONS. It is also important to learn to remove oneself from emotional situations without distancing. This means being present during conflict in the cross-generational context and learning to observe how family dynamics work to put a person back into the roles of childhood. Family members often seek, unwittingly or intentionally, to draw the person back into the old family dynamics as a way of lessening tension and conflict. Resistance to being drawn in by noting the pressure but not submitting to it is called extricating oneself from family dynamics. Through this extricating process, the person can stay connected to the family in a healthy way.

Applying Reconnection Skills

Using the methods just described to connect with the family of origin and to honor parents is essential for adult children who have had difficulty developing self-differentiation for themselves. These methods honor parents primarily because they lend themselves to maintaining relationships in ways that promote the well-being of both adult children and their parents. Such methods of self-differentiation put the adult child in an emotional position to accept the reversal of roles between generations in the event that aging parents become dependent. In other words, self-differentiation is a prerequisite to the reversal of roles between adult children and aging dependent parents, and these methods promote the achievement of the self-differentiation requirements.

The following case demonstrates how these methods have been employed. Betsey always had difficulty being herself around her parents. When with her parents, she would blend in with what was going on and assume the roles she took as a child. She hated doing this but felt she had no real alternatives. She also found herself blending in with others, particularly in close relationships. She also harbored feelings of resentment: she felt that people really did not know her or respect her.

At her parents' home, Betsey was often dragged into the middle of her parents' marital problems. She did not know how to get out of this uncomfortable bind. If she took sides with one parent, she would alienate the other. She tried to stay out of their problems, but she was always being caught in the cross fire.

Betsey mastered the techniques of extricating herself from family dynamics and learned to employ them when she went home. She made sure that she had time alone with each parent, and she was careful to avoid conversations about the other parent. This gradually improved and deepened her relationship with each parent. She felt more in charge of herself and less vulnerable to being drawn into her parents' marital problems.

By daring to become self-differentiated, Betsey laid the foundation for honoring her parents. At one stage of the developmental cycle, honoring parents requires becoming self-differentiated. This self-differentiation lays the groundwork for later phases of the life cycle when honoring means seeing to it that aging parents who have lost their independence are cared for.

Concluding Commentary

Cross-generational relationships have been important survival mechanisms for African Americans. This chapter has explored these relationships and how honoring elders helps to recapture the legacy of this mechanism for the benefit of all. It has also emphasized that honoring elders and enriching the lives of younger generations are promoted by maintaining cross-generational contact. The family genogram was offered as an aid in the process of reconnecting with the extended family, especially with family elders. Persons who engage in family genogram work do so to arrive at a picture of the family as a whole, as well as to determine ways of working through relational issues.

This chapter has emphasized that skills and techniques help mediate a balance between self-differentiation, or the normal separation of maturing adults from their families, and mature connectedness. These skills and techniques are employed in a process called "returning home," and include building person-to-person relationships with family members, controlling emotional reactivity, and extricating oneself from emotional situations.

Question for Reflection

How would you complete a genogram? Use Figure 6.1 to help you construct a three-generational family genogram. Begin with your own generation. If you are married, use the symbol for marriage and indicate your wedding date. Include your age and your spouse's age. If you have children, use the symbols and indicate the names and birth dates of each child. Include information under "Kinds of Information to Seek," if applicable. Then add the same information about your parents, if applicable.

If you are single, the three-generational family could be you and your siblings, parents, and grandparents. Include information asked for under "Kinds of Information to Seek," if applicable.

CREATING ELDER MINISTRIES FOR DIFFERENT LOCATIONS

Stephen C. Rasor

MRS. P AND MRS. R MET for the first time at a regional church meeting. Both elders are in their seventies and are active in their local congregations. They took particular interest in the regional meeting because of its focus on seniors. As part of the event, the elders shared parts of their stories with a partner to highlight the needs of elders. The two women discovered quite soon that they lived in very different locations but had many things in common.

In sharing her story, Mrs. P said: "I was born and raised in the country. My daddy had a farm, and all of my brothers and sisters worked on it. Everybody worked hard. But we had plenty to eat. I love the country. There is nothing like it. It's beautiful, fresh, and clean.

"I raised my own family in a small town. They've all moved quite a distance away. My husband died a few years ago. Many of my family and friends have passed on, too. But I've got a sister and a brother up the road, and we keep up with each other. Their children don't live too far away either, and they stop in every now and again and help me take care of things around the house. Still, sometimes I worry about being a burden on them.

"The older I get, the harder some things seem to be. It's hard living alone and getting around to take care of those everyday things. My doctor is in the next county. I have to get a ride to go there.

Somebody has to take me to the grocery, too. My sister and brother are not young by any means. And, well, young folk need to live their own lives. I feel beholden sometimes.

"I don't see my children and grandchildren near enough. But I understand. I wish they lived closer by. Summers are special times, though, because that's when they come. Sometimes one grandchild or another spends a week or two.

"Oh, I have my church. I so enjoy my church. Our preacher is a good man. He visits regular. He made sure I got to this meeting. He's always talking about looking after your own. There's not a lot of young folk there. But my church is my family too. I'm so glad to have it. Anyway, that's my story. When it's all said and done, I wouldn't want to move from where I live for anything!"

Mrs. R joined in the conversation by saying that she couldn't agree more with some of the things Mrs. P was saying even though she grew up and still lived in the "big city." She said: "My father came from the country to work in the city and stayed. I was one of four children born in the city. I met and married my husband there. He and I had to struggle. Raising our boys was tough. But they've done OK for themselves.

My husband passed ten years ago. I've stayed in the same house. Before he died, my boys had already left to go on with their lives in another state. They get home for Christmas and pretty near every summer. I miss their not being here all the time. But one of my sisters lives across town, and I see her pretty often.

People in my Sunday school class pick me up most every Sunday. I've been going to the same church for years and years. I wouldn't have gotten to this meeting if one of the class members hadn't let me ride with him. I feel good at my church. They love me and I love them. God has been good to me. Some of the younger church folk come by to see me quite often. They call and ask if I need anything. They're good about making sure I have transportation. I used to take the bus all the time. But with my arthritis, it's not so easy anymore. And you know, I'm a little bit afraid with the crime situation. Sometimes, though, I don't have a choice. Sometimes I just have to take the bus in order to get where I need to go."

○

Engaging in honor-bestowing ministry with and on behalf of elders requires our awareness of the variety of locations in which they live. This ministry presupposes as well our concern for the well-being of elders in various contexts and our response to threats to their well-being.

In Chapter Four, we were reminded that elders reside in rural and metropolitan areas. The stories of Mrs. P and Mrs. R at the beginning of this chapter draw our attention again to these areas and to common and unique challenges elders face within them. Their stories also tell us that the role of the church is important to them.

The intent in this chapter is to consider situations of elders in rural and metropolitan areas and matters concerning their well-being about which we should be aware in our practice of ministry. Moreover, the purpose is to propose a range of context-specific responses that churches might give to these matters. We will begin by clarifying the meaning of rural and metropolitan areas.

A View of Rural and Metropolitan Areas

Rural areas have been variously defined by the U.S. Bureau of the Census as ranging from nonmetropolitan counties, which could have cities of up to fifty thousand people, to towns in the open countryside with twenty-five hundred or fewer residents (Flora, Flora, Spears, and Swanson, 1992). However, rural areas tend to be more diverse than population figures alone portray. As a geographically defined locality, they are better understood as nonmetropolitan areas characterized by small populations, sparse settlements, and remoteness. Rural areas encompass farm and nonfarm, old and new areas (Muchow, 1993; Koff, 1992).

Koff (1992) also points out that rural communities are defined by their cultural qualities. These qualities include a long history of family residence, historically strong community ties, and ethnic cultural attachments. Rural communities are further defined by their growing number of elderly persons. Overall, approximately 29 percent of older Americans live in rural areas. Of these elders, 91 percent live in rural small towns and settlements or in nonfarm open country. In numerous counties, the overall proportion of older rural Americans above age sixty-five reaches almost 20 percent of the population compared to the national average of around 12 percent (McCulloch, 1995; Flora, Flora, Spears, and Swanson, 1992).

We tend to think of older African American men and women residing in' the large metropolitan areas. But 42 percent of them actually live in rural areas (Bone, 1991). Though the nation experienced a great shift in population between 1900 and 1980, many African

American elders remained in the rural parts of the country, especially in the South.

Standard metropolitan areas (SMAs) are defined by the Census Bureau as a single county or a group of counties having at least one central city of fifty thousand or more residents. These areas also feature great geographical diversity. This diversity is evident in the observable central core or inner city, a surrounding circle of neighborhoods, and business sectors of the urban area of the metropolis. Metropolitan areas are identified additionally by their further removed suburban sectors.

People are connected in metropolitan areas by residential patterns, often along ethnic cultural lines, and they form friendships and close ties within the neighborhoods where they reside. Nearly one-third of all noninstitutionalized persons aged sixty-five and over live in the central core of urban areas, and the remainder reside in the suburbs. We find the greatest number of African Americans in the inner core of metropolitan areas (Skinner, 1992).

Life of African American Elders in the Rural Context

Older African American residents of rural areas have strong communal ties, personal strengths, and perseverance they have developed over their lifetimes. These qualities are worthy of recognition and affirmation within the churches they attend. They also face special threats to their well-being, which call for responses from our churches.

Poverty

They experience persistent poverty due to a lifetime of disadvantages such as high unemployment rates and lower educational attainment. Moreover, poverty is a particularly significant issue. In rural areas, the poverty rate is nearly 50 percent (Harper and Alexander, 1990). It is even higher—nearly 80 percent—among African American women living alone in areas beyond the city and suburbs (Bone, 1991; Muchow, 1993).

Poor Health

Poor health is also a major issue among rural African Americans. These elders have a significantly higher rate of diabetes (55 percent) than white elders do. A majority (60 percent) of the African

American diabetic population lives in southern states, where the greatest number of rural African American elders live. These elders also suffer in great numbers from hypertension, cancer, and musculoskeletal disorders (Bone, 1991).

Transportation Issues

Limited transportation magnifies the isolation and erects geographical barriers for many rural elders. This is no less the case with rural African American elders, as noted in the opening story. As a result, elders experience restricted access to the already limited numbers of health professionals and community-based programs.

The transportation issue is compounded by the reality that many of the younger men and women have moved out of the rural areas, as also noted in the opening story. These younger family members leave the rural environment because of limits in education and employment. But their elders are unlikely to migrate from their familiar surroundings. Many elders, like Mrs. P in the opening story, live alone. In this situation, the elders cannot always afford vehicles; nor are they always able to drive themselves. Studies indicate that the informal support systems provided by younger generations in rural areas are stronger among African Americans than other Americans. However, we need to be aware of the very real impact the out-migration of younger family members has on access to needed services (Bone, 1991; Koff, 1992).

Substandard Housing

We need to be aware of other issues faced by some rural elders, including African Americans, such as substandard housing, difficulties in maintaining repairs, lack of plumbing, no central heating, and no telephone service (Koff, 1992). In the opening story, Mrs. P relied on the children of her sister and brother to help her in matters pertaining to her house. However, not every elder has access to such assistance. And congregations who might offer or find assistance may not be fully aware of housing issues faced by nonattending or homebound elders.

Special Issues of the Frail Elderly

Rural individuals eighty-five years of age and older have certain special needs. These "frail elderly" have increased in recent years. They are mostly women, quite poor, and fairly isolated. They tend to live alone. Their ability to perform even basic domestic activities is diminished. As indicated earlier, having family members close by to help with cooking, cleaning, and transportation has become less the case in recent years. The "increasing out-migration of young people from rural communities means that many elderly are left without family support and only moderate neighbor support" (Flora, Flora, Spears, and Swanson, 1992, p. 279). This is certainly true for many rural African American elders.

Family, Community, and Church Responses

Rural elders rely on an intergenerational network of relatives and friends and intragenerational supports from other elders in times of need (Taylor, 1988). This informal helping network provides "affective and/or instrumental" supports. Love and understanding, which contribute to necessary emotional well-being, are affective support ingredients. Housecleaning, transportation, food, and money are all forms of instrumental support. In the opening story, Mrs. P relied heavily on her elderly sister and brother and their children.

But rural elders, their families, and their neighbors also tend to rely on voluntary associations such as the church rather than local government to assist them. Elders themselves look to the church as a place for social cohesion, support, and resourceful contribution. Sometimes small rural congregations are not regarded as vital churches because of the large proportion of elders in them. We must move from this view to one that recognizes a church as vital whenever it provides meaningful and helpful activities for its members and responds to their needs and desires.

Rural churches may take responsibility for meals-on-wheels programs and the provision of basic supplies for the indigent. During times of illness, elders and their families rely on the church for home visits, prayers, Holy Communion from the pastor, and other supports, such as food (Watson, 1990; Flora, Flora, Spears, and Swanson, 1992). However, systematic visitation is particularly important regardless of whether elders are ailing. We show our care for elders through this personal presence with them. And we discover their needs, how they feel about their situations, and what they and family members want us to do.

The task of the rural church is not always easy. This is especially true for small churches because much must be done by a few people.

Giving an adequate response requires the pastor's vigilance to the needs that arise, willingness to get involved, and readiness to mobilize already identified resources. The task may be more easily undertaken when churches develop partnerships with other churches within the same locale. Pastors may also encourage congregations to collaborate with formal helping agencies. These contacts might include county extension programs, existing senior centers, the Red Cross, and the Area Agency on Aging for speakers, technical assistance, information and referral, and other supports to address identified needs.

Life of African American Elders in the Metropolis

In the opening story, we became aware of Mrs. R.'s worries about getting around on buses with her arthritis and her concern for safety and maintaining her home. "Tee" and "Em" (not their real names) are two other elders who reside in a metropolitan area. At one time, these sisters were quite independent and mobile in their activities. But now, like so many other seniors, they choose not to go out at night. Most of their activity takes place during the daylight hours. Unfortunately, their poor health has also greatly limited even daytime activity. They find themselves increasingly separated from the range of church activities they love. Many urban elders are like Tee and Em.

Many of the problems we highlighted in our description of rural life can be seen in metropolitan areas. We find in urban areas similar issues of poverty. Overall, one-third of African American elders are poor, and many additional elders are classified as "near poor" (Harper and Alexander, 1990). We also find issues of ill health, inadequate housing, and difficult access to needed services. The urban environment, combined with aging processes and concerns, contributes to a particular kind of vulnerability for many African American elders.

Urban Elders' Vulnerability

A significant number of older African Americans live in the central cores of urban areas or inner cities where poverty and crime create a troublesome environment. Although in lesser numbers than other Americans, frail African American elders also reside in institutional settings.

ENVIRONMENTAL PROBLEMS. Urban elders often live in environments typified by dilapidated housing, poor lighting, bad sidewalks, inaccessible stairs, and various barriers to needed transportation, medical, and social services. We also find in these areas numbers of unemployed persons and school dropouts. And the urban elders tend to have few other residential options. They have in the past experienced discrimination and poverty. Now, in their elder years, they find they must endure threats to their personal dignity, security, and overall well-being (Biegel and Farkas, 1990; Watson, 1991). They are vulnerable to victimization.

CRIME. Crime is one of the primary concerns of urban elderly women and men. Being a victim of crime is an everyday worry. The homicide rate has increased among persons fifty-five years of age and older. This increase is greater among elders than any other age group. Larceny, physical assault, purse snatching, and other crimes are problems older people, especially African Americans, face regularly (Watson, 1991).

As a result, older men and women tend to stay inside their homes in a kind of self-imposed house arrest. Their sense of isolation and loneliness is compounded by their fear of venturing beyond their doors. They don't want to go outside. Their immediate surroundings feed their need to protect themselves, and their efforts toward self-protection increase their sense of isolation and victimization.

Mr. H is an elder who lives in a high-crime urban area. His retirement income is such that he can live nowhere else. He stays to himself much of the time since he was taunted by a group of teenagers on his way to a neighborhood store. He became increasingly withdrawn after this incident. He is reluctant to go out because of his fear of being victimized by younger people in his neighborhood and becomes depressed due to his restricted human contact. Mr. H is similar to many elderly city dwellers.

INSTITUTIONALIZED ELDERS. Approximately 3 percent of all African American elderly reside in institutional settings, compared to about 5 percent of other Americans. These residents are typically the oldest old (aged eighty-five and over) who are widowed, childless, or single. Approximately 12 percent of African American elders aged eighty-five and over reside in nursing homes, compared to 23 percent other Americans of that age (Harper and Alexander, 1990). These elders often have very small family and friend networks; consequently, these elders are at risk of becoming "invisible" to churches and "out of bounds" to their ministry. Although nursing homes exist in rural areas, most are in metropolitan areas.

Incarcerated Elders

Another urban problem in more recent years is an increase in elderly men and women committing crimes themselves. The criminality of older persons is on the way up. This is not a topic that receives much attention, but there is evidence to indicate that this is the case. Watson (1991) reports that quarrels among associates, alcohol abuse, and general frustration have increased violence and criminality among older citizens. "In regard to homicides committed by older persons, they tend to follow a quarrel between persons who are very familiar with each other and tend to occur in relatively private places. Murder-suicides are especially likely under conditions of previously long-term intimate relations spoiled by terminal illness of one or both partners. Less fatal forms of elder abuse, such as assault and battery and financial exploitation, may also occur under these conditions" (p. 56).

Elders who commit crimes also face incarceration. In entering the prison system, they join other imprisoned elders, many of whom are long-term prisoners. African Americans are disproportionately represented in this group, as they are in the total prison population.

For incarcerated elders, the prison atmosphere with younger inmates is often problematic. Generational differences cause difficulty in communication. Elder prisoners themselves often become vulnerable to negative treatment by other inmates or are confined to designated quarters because of debilitating conditions such as diabetes, arthritis, amputations, and blindness. Many confront the reality of their incarceration and the mistakes they have made and issues related to their aging, health, self-esteem, and boredom.

Not much is done by way of prison ministry that targets them. When it does occur, it provides unknown assistance, owing to the tendency of this ministry to be done by part-time persons and volunteers who are not fully prepared for it. Although these "special" elders are unrepresentative of society's elders, they reside in a setting where ministry is needed nonetheless; indeed, prison can become a "unique parish" (Graham, 1990; James Gray, Prison Fellowship International, personal interview, 1996).

Elder Abuse

Maltreated elders form a special subgroup of elders in which we find African Americans. Two points are of importance with reference to them. First, elders who are abused do not necessarily acknowledge their abuse; nor do they always report it when they acknowledge it. This is because, typically, the abuser is a family member. But in our relations with elders, especially as part of a visitation ministry, we may see the effects of abuse. Second, abused elders often need encouragement to take necessary steps toward safety, and they need help in locating specialized psychosocial support personnel in order to address their situation (Qualls, 1995).

Challenges to Elders in Multigenerational Households

Because of the financial insufficiencies and economic challenges of elders as well as family members, elders are more likely than their rural counterparts to live in extended family households. This allows them to pool resources and engage in other reciprocal helping activities (Lockery, 1991). But more than this, increasing numbers of African American elders are becoming surrogate parents to grandchildren and great-grandchildren. Currently, 12 percent of African American children reside with a grandparent or great-grandparent. As an outgrowth of these intergenerational living arrangements, elders experience advantages, rewards, and joy. But they also experience challenges with which they need help (Burton and Devries, 1992).

The life cycle and cross-generational processes introduced in the two preceding chapters are helpful in addressing family relations in these contexts. However, older adult ministry may increasingly be called on to provide further creative solutions to multiple issues arising in these situations. Burton and Devries's (1992) study targets the uncertainty that grandparents have about the ability and longevity they need to raise young children. Their uncertainty is accentuated when they take on responsibility not only for newborns but also for several children of varying ages (p. 53). Burton and Devries also show that elders have difficulty keeping up physically with children in school, social, and recreational activities, and that they struggle with not having the know-how to guide children in contemporary school homework. Regardless of their location, grandparents tell stories that confirm these researchers' findings. A widowed grandmother attended a series of family cluster project meetings for single parents and their children at the Interdenominational Theological Center. The 1994 project was designed to provide support and to enhance family relationships and communication through shared story. At one of the meetings, the grandmother shared the following:

> I felt pulled in many directions when I was raising my own children. I had to help them with their homework, take them to their activities, go to the P.T.A. meetings, and keep up with all the other things on the home front. But I was young then. Now I don't have the energy I once had. Things have changed in the school too. I discovered there's something called the "new math." I actually had to get some tutoring myself in order to help my two grandchildren. They say you're never too old to learn. Well, I'm proving that's true. At least I'm hoping that I'm helping my grandbabies by what I'm able to learn. But now I've got a question. Do they say you can keep up with these youngsters when you get to be my age? I'm not sure I'm going to prove that. But God knows I'm doing the best I can.

Increasingly, elderly adults are also taking care of their still older parents or relatives. This situation can severely tax the elder caregiver. It raises significant concern for the well-being of both sets of elders. Clearly, elders who are either surrogate parents or caregivers of still older relatives need assistance in these matters.

Elders with Favorable Benefit Systems

Much of the research on African American elders focuses dominantly on those who have unfavorable benefit systems. That is, attention is given primarily to elders who face multiple socioeconomic deficits and health challenges. We need to recognize, however, that there is a group of elders who have accumulated income and other assets, benefits, and pensions. They have adequate housing, cultivate a variety of interests, and are typically engaged in a variety of self-selected retirement pursuits, from personal enrichment to intragenerational and intergenerational service activities. These elders are found mostly in urban and suburban areas.

Like other elders, these elders face health problems and relocation when debilitating illness strikes or a spouse dies. Like other elders, they sometimes confront difficult decisions with respect to life and death issues. Some of them become surrogate parents to grandchildren and great-grandchildren. Some become caregivers for still older relatives. Even though they and the informal networks to which they are connected are more apt to know where to get help when needed, they, too, can find themselves in a quandary. They look to the church for social cohesion, participation in church life, information, spiritual growth, and service opportunities.

In sum, urban life presents challenges to elders' well-being and opportunities for churches to contribute to their well-being. There is need for us to respond and coordinate our efforts with the elders' identified needs, their families, and community agencies.

Family, Neighborhood, and Church Responses

To varying degrees, metropolitan elders, like rural elders, receive support from other elders and from younger relatives and neighborhood friends. But metropolitan-area churches are particularly important agents in providing a range of programs that respond to elders' needs to be receivers of help and contributors to church life. In many cases, family members, by virtue of their church membership, become links to services provided by churches. But this may not happen for elders who are childless, whose relatives do not attend church, or who themselves have become "invisible" to churches due to advanced age, nonattendance, or disabling conditions (Taylor, 1988). Churches have a signal opportunity to seek out elders wherever they are and to ascertain and respond to their needs.

The responses of churches must vary according to their size and resources and the needs of elders. But there are three categories of responses all churches can undertake. First, as in rural areas, an essential ongoing part of the ministry is systematic visitation wherever elders reside. We respond best to elders' needs when we remain in contact with them. Both clergy and lay visitation teams need to undertake this ministry initiative.

Second, metropolitan areas typically have a complex system of social supports about which elders and family members are not always aware or which they have difficulty accessing. An important role of the church is identifying these supports and serving as a mediating structure between elders and the formal helping structures (Berger, 1977). We will explore ways to build a collaborative church and community helping network in Chapter Eight.

Finally, churches can and must be carers and advocates on behalf of elders. Indeed, doing so continues a key historical element of "soul" in African American cultural and religious expression, as indicated in the opening chapter and throughout Part One of this book. Our churches respond best when we consider what we can successfully do from a ministry continuum that includes options:

- From elder housing maintenance task forces, food pantries, and financial contingency funds for assuring elders' basic supplies to church-sponsored housing
- From elder companions and transportation supports for physically challenged elders and those in high-crime areas to advocating for greater availability of public transportation, crime watches, and other neighborhood safety improvements
- From offering support structures for families in elder care-giving situations to assistance to families facing difficult life and death decisions
- From acknowledging the reality that elder abuse does occur to offering workshops on what it is and what to do about it
- From discovering allowable ways of engaging in prison ministry with elder inmates and providing skills preparation through organizations such as Prison Fellowship USA to carrying out the actual ministry in selected locations
- From identifying grandparents and great-grandparents in surrogate parent roles to forming creative programs focused on respite or "time out" for these elders, including parallel activities for them and the children
- From church-based activities to community outreach initiatives that assure helpful responses to and resourceful participation of a diverse group of elders

Assuring a Soul Community Among Elders in Different Locations

One of the themes that runs through this book is the affirmation of a basic and absolutely necessary element of the African American church experience: soul. We have discovered that solidarity is the pivotal descriptor of soul that permeates congregational initiatives designed to honor elders and ensure their well-being. When we take seriously the variety of responses in rural and metropolitan areas mentioned earlier in the chapter, we exercise the meaning of the church as a soul community.

There are numerous instances where congregations already function as soul communities by virtue of their ministry with and on behalf of elders. But clearly, more churches must be more vigilant in our present situation of expanding numbers of elders and their growing needs. We can be encouraged, however, by specific church and parachurch exemplars of older adult ministry.

Church Exemplars

There are many examples of African American churches that are making older adult ministry happen. We will look at just two, one in a rural area and the other in an urban context, that serve as models of the church as a soul community.

VALLEY QUEEN BAPTIST CHURCH, MARKS, MISSISSIPPI. This church is a rural congregation with approximately two hundred members that serves its community, including the elderly. Under the pastoral leadership of Dr. Carl Brown, Valley Queen has contributed significantly to the well-being of elders in this rural setting.

The church provides a nutritionally balanced meal for approximately sixty elders on a daily basis. This creative feeding program both meets the needs of the hungry and addresses the issue of loneliness. God's love and care are shown in tangible ways through food and fellowship. The church also has a nursing home visitation program. This program entails regular visits to these facilities for purposes of providing emotional, spiritual, and social supports to the residents. The program is funded by the church and staffed by volunteers (Burt and Roper, 1992; Billingsley, 1992).

ALLEN AFRICAN METHODIST EPISCOPAL CHURCH, QUEENS, NEW YORK. This church of three thousand members has contributed significantly to the well-being of elders through its extensive community outreach ministry. Under the leadership of Rev. Floyd Flake, this church responds to the needs of older men and women in the New York City borough of Queens. A senior citizen housing program, Allen Senior Citizens Community Center, and the Allen Home Care Agency are but three of many initiatives that exemplify the meaning of solidarity.

The church assures a safe, healthy, and affordable urban environment in its housing program. The housing complex makes the approximately 325 resident seniors feel at home. The church's senior citizen community center enables elders to enjoy one another's company in recreational, social, and food-related activities. The Allen Home Care Agency reaches homebound elders. It reportedly serves nearly three hundred persons (Billingsley, 1992).

Parachurch Organizations

Parachurch organizations are religious structures that operate outside local church and denominational bounds. They typically relate directly with churches to carry out a broad range of activities that many congregations cannot provide on their own. One organization of this type is Reaching Out to Senior Adults (ROSA) in Atlanta, Georgia. This organization was mentioned in the opening story in Chapter Four.

ROSA was organized in 1988 by four Georgia State University students who sought to enhance the lives of elders. The organization provides programs and a network for meeting the spiritual needs and improving the quality of life for senior adults. It serves as an umbrella group for chapters of senior adults that form in local congregations.

The chapters meet within the local churches and as a total group once each month. Each chapter determines its own purpose, its ministry description, and how it will operate. The monthly meetings for all ROSA chapters provide inspirational and educational presentations by clergy, health care professionals and other social service providers, legislators, and seniors themselves.

The organization also hosts a citywide annual breakfast, special worship services, and an outreach day. The outreach day event presents exhibits, information booths on leisure, health and community services, health screening, and health promotion workshops to focus attention on elder self-care. Counseling stations provide in-depth counseling about Social Security programs, Medicare, and Medicaid.

In addition to these citywide events, ROSA provides leadership training events to assist churches in developing and finding resources to support senior ministry and building intergenerational components to their ministry. A part of ROSA's ongoing efforts is helping older persons access agencies, organizations, and service providers in the community. The executive director is Rev. Normal Phillips.

Ensuring Elder Input and Participation

Older adults themselves have said that "we must be part of the planning for anything involving us. . . . Who else will know what is really right for us?" (A. S. Wimberly, 1991). This admonition of our elders is instructive for what must happen if our churches are to be soul communities that carry out a ministry *with* and not simply to them. This means seeking their advice, including them on planning committees, and involving them in the implementation of programming.

Whether in rural or metropolitan areas, the church community and others beyond it are enriched by the contributions of elders. An example of the enriching activity of elders is found in the story of retirees Charles and Jane. This couple had been in full-time ministry prior to retirement. In retirement, they continued to do everything humanly possible to make life better for others in their neighborhood, their church, and the urban community where they lived. Prison ministry, literacy action, ministry in public housing projects, and general advocacy for justice were their everyday concerns. Until they died, they prayed to, worshiped, and served Jesus as part of their so-called retired existence.

The couple continued as leaders in the congregation with which they became affiliated. They were revered by the children, youth, and adults. They were known as models of what Christians were supposed to be and do. The members often invoked their names. They didn't fear death. They didn't regret retirement. They never saw themselves as useless. They were examples of repositories of wisdom and resourceful contributors to a community that comprised "Christian elderhood." They honored Christ, they honored themselves, and the members honored them. The church honors them still.

The story of this couple reminds us of the imperative responsibility of the church as a soul community, whatever its location, to take seriously the wisdom of our elders and take advantage of their years. The church can and must celebrate old age not as a curse, as sometimes is the case, but as a blessing from God. Clergy and laity alike have a signal opportunity to model their reverence and support of Christian elderhood. But it really starts with the local church leadership. And it will not materialize independent of intentional ministry effort.

In worship we must teach, preach, and showcase a liturgy that reaffirms Christian elderhood. Our worship must lay the spiritual and theological foundation for the honoring of our elders. We worship a God who honors us all, especially those who have been on the journey of faith longer than most.

Our church school, confirmation training, and Bible study must underscore a practical theology that honors our seniors. They teach and we learn. We show our youth what Christian discipleship means by acquainting them with our Christian senior mentors. We take them seriously and teach honor and respect.

We must train our laity to respond to the affective and instrumental needs of our seniors. We must first teach ourselves to listen. Listening with great interest to our elder men and women shows them great respect. We honor them and value them when we sit and listen to their stories.

Finally, we must create programs of service that enable young and old, teenagers and elders, to work side by side in providing ministry to others. As we often minister to others, in the name of Jesus Christ, we will rediscover one another. As we respect and honor others, we honor each other—and ourselves. Intergenerational service to others brings us together. It allows our soul to reemerge. It accentuates our soul community. Regardless of location, ministry with and on behalf of our elders happens when we plan for it to happen. We make it happen when we consistently ask for whom, with whom, for what, and by when must we act, when we set our action in motion, and when we secure accountability structures to ensure our success. Our starting place is to examine our own situation (Dudley, 1991). We must get to it.

Concluding Commentary

This chapter has attempted to highlight ways we can honor our elders in rural and metropolitan environments. These two environments have common features as well as distinctive ones. Both have a need for intentional responses to a variety of conditions that threaten the well-being of elders. They also have responses that family, neighborhoods, and churches already provide but must continue to contribute to their well-being. The distinctive feature of rural isolation and the distinctive features of elder vulnerability in the face of urban complexity and crime require attention.

Churches can and must assume responsibility alone and in collaboration with community agencies to minister with and on behalf of elders on the basis of the elders' needs and the churches' resources. To do so honors the elders, brings honor to the churches, and confirms them as soul communities.

Questions for Reflection

1. Who are the elderly among you? What are their names?
2. Where are they living? What are their addresses, their neighborhoods, and characteristics of their living environments that may be troubling?

3. How are they living? Do they live alone, with a spouse, or with other relatives? Do they have the basic supplies for living?

4. What are their special gifts?

5. What are their special needs?

6. Who is presently giving and receiving among the older people in your church? What is the nature of their giving and receiving, and how is it regarded by the church?

7. How can the elderly help you and others do ministry?

8. What do you need to do to begin new initiatives or continue old ones in your ministry with and on behalf of elders?

9. Where specifically will you start in your efforts to begin new initiatives? What will you do to assess old ones for their effectiveness?

10. How do you anticipate experiencing God in the lives of those whom you serve?

BUILDING
A HELPING NETWORK

Anne Streaty Wimberly

ON ONE SIDE OF TOWN, Mrs. L, a seventy-eight-year-old widow, lives in a small bungalow that has been home for at least fifty years. She and her husband raised two girls in that home, and she tells stories to her grandchildren there. Her husband died in that home. Her memories and the fact that the home is paid for keep her there. But Mrs. L's meager pension makes it difficult for her to make repairs. Keeping up with utilities and other bills is also a problem. She says that her girls have helped along the way, but they are struggling with their own bills and raising children. She said that some of her friends who live in a senior high-rise told her to give it up, but she refuses to leave her home, she says, "as long as I'm in my right mind." But she admits, "I haven't figured out how I'm going to handle things."

On another street not far from Mrs. L, Mrs. M, aged thirty-seven, and her three children, aged seven, twelve, and thirteen, have lived with her father for four years. Mrs. M had been divorced for a year when she moved to her father's home. He had just retired on disability after suffering kidney failure and beginning dialysis three times weekly. Mrs. M's mother died of breast cancer when she was in her mid-fifties. Living with her father helped Mrs. M financially, and it gave her father some needed supports. For some time after she moved in, Mrs. M was able to juggle her schedule with the children and work in a way that allowed her to take her father for dialysis.

But when she changed jobs, she was no longer able to do it. She struggled to find transportation for him. She said she finally found it through "calling this place and that place." In addition, her father's health problems have increased to the point where he needs daily living assistance that Mrs. M doesn't have time to give. She said, "Now, where am I going to turn for this?"

Mr. and Mrs. R reside in a comfortable home in another neighborhood. Mr. R is a retired teacher; Mrs. R is still teaching. Mr. R described himself as being in good health and always looking for ways to keep active. Both are active in their church, mostly on weekends. Mrs. R suggested a senior center or another kind of senior program, but they have had difficulty finding ones that meet their needs.

o

As people enter and move through their elder years, they face an array of issues. In Chapter Seven, we were introduced to some of the issues seniors face in rural and metropolitan areas. The opening stories in this chapter also revealed particular kinds of problems of elders and the people who care for them.

A network of services is available in the public domain to help elders and their caregivers with various everyday issues. However, the elders do not always know the public agencies, programs, and services that are available to them and how to access them. And those who assist them on an informal basis are often unaware of the variety of services that can help them manage the task of caregiving. Yet the highest possible quality and efficiency of care of elders depends on accessing this formal resource network.

A part of the church's responsibility as the soul community is to bring the network of services to the awareness of elders and the people caring for them and to assist them all in accessing it. Doing this is part of our way of showing our solidarity with the elders and our honor of them. It is an important and valid part of our ministry with and on behalf of elders. But what exactly can we as a soul community do to connect elders and informal helpers with public agencies, programs, and services to which elders are entitled? What are some services and agencies in the public domain of which we should be aware? What is the soul community's role as a helper among helpers? In the following sections, we will explore answers to these questions.

The Soul Community as a Network Builder

It is important for the church as a soul community to be a network builder. Our churches are second to the network of family and friends as dominant caregiving institutions for elders (Martin and Martin, 1985; Taylor, 1986, 1988; Billingsley, 1992). As noted in Chapter Seven, our churches are mediating structures that exist between the family and the public domain. As such, they have the opportunity to connect persons with supportive resources. In this way, the church as a soul community may be called an "opportunity structure." Our recognition of this role is a necessary first preparatory task to connecting elders and their helpers with formal resources.

Second, it is important as well for us to recognize the pivotal role of the clergy and church older adult ministry leaders in carrying out the mediating role of the church as a soul community. These persons are the trusted advisers to whom elders and their caregivers should be able to turn for information and guidance. Their acknowledgment of the church's role as a network builder and their intentionality in learning the network are pivotal preparatory tasks to disseminating information about it.

A third preparatory task is our becoming aware of what, precisely, being a "network builder" means and what key activities must be undertaken to build a helping network. It is to this matter that we now turn.

A Helping Network: What It Is and How to Build It

A helping network is a constellation of important relationships forged between our churches and helpers in the public domain who provide assistance, support, and guidance for living aimed toward enhancing the well-being of elders. An identifiable, accessible, and functioning network is a resource that allows us to carry on our ministry toward elders' well-being in a fuller manner than is possible without it. Through the cooperative efforts we forge with public agencies, we help make known God's presence and grace. In this way, we honors elders.

Building a helping network takes intentional effort on our part. Effort is needed to identify and connect with public agencies and programs whose goals are to benefit elders and family helpers. Effort is also needed to identify older members and families needing help and to disseminate to them information about available resources and how to access them.

Activities for Building a Helping Network

Here we will consider activities that help us in our network building. The activities are organized in three phases: readiness activities, activities of initiation, and follow-up activities.

PHASE ONE: READINESS. Older adult ministry leaders form the human and information resources needed to begin an intentional process of building a helping network.

1. *Create an older adult ministry team whose responsibility is to build a helping network.* Make an appeal for team members who are interested in and committed to building such a network. These persons may include elders and family members who have gone through processes of locating needed support services. These persons already have some knowledge about the network and ways of accessing it. As a result, they may be strong advocates for network building. Team members may also include persons who are in the process of seeking support services and who, as a result, are highly motivated to identify service agencies, programs, and resources. In addition, include on the team, or in an advisory capacity, any professionals who are connected with social service agencies. These persons have expertise in guiding the process of network building.

2. *Emphasize the need to invest time in developing the helping network.* Let the team members know that they will need to spend time contacting elders and relatives of elders to discern their present needs for help. They will need to take time to identify specific areas in which helpers are needed as well as to identify potential needs based in part on what they have learned from elders and family members. They will have to spend time locating aging network information and referral telephone numbers. They will have to spend time discovering whether city, county, or state aging services have information handbooks or other written materials that list available services.

3. *Send for available reference materials.* Collect city, county, or state aging services information handbooks or other written materials that list available services. These materials serve as reference tools and prevent us from engaging in an unnecessary search for service providers. These materials also prevent us from duplicating services.

4. *Create a file of names of agencies, resources, and materials.* Include descriptions and information on where and how to access them. Establish who will maintain the organization of the file and who will provide elders and family members with information from it.

5. *Build a resource library.* Collect resource books, pamphlets, brochures, and other materials, and place them in a location that is open to elders and family members. Establish who will maintain the resources and supervise their use.

PHASE TWO: INITIATION. Older adult ministry teams decide and complete key strategies and practical steps needed to make a helping network come alive.

1. *Announce the helping network.* Make the soul community's establishment of a helping network known publicly through church bulletins, newsletters, and telephone and personal contacts. Let everyone know of the existence of a resource library and where and how to make use of it.

2. *Establish a speakers' forum.* Invite ministry team members to highlight the helping network at special meetings. Also invite local service agency personnel to speak at forums for elders and their families on topics and services in their areas of expertise.

3. *Provide names and contact numbers of helpers to elders and family members.* Use the file and resource library to provide information about helpers needed by elders and family members. Use volunteers to assist elders who need help in contacting service agencies in the public domain.

PHASE THREE: FOLLOW-UP. Older adult ministry teams monitor helping network functions, assessing network appropriateness and effectiveness, and facilitating access to the network by the greatest possible number of elders and their families.

1. *Link with other churches.* Join or form a consortium of churches in establishing an interdenominational and regional helping network initiative. Great amounts of information may be pooled and a wider number of elders and family members may be reached through collective efforts.

2. *Evaluate your efforts.* Contact elders and family who have made use of the helping network ministry for feedback on its value, its effectiveness, and areas of needed change or improvement. Also, continue contacts with elders and family members within and beyond the soul community to discover emerging needs for helpers.

3. *Keep development going.* Adjust the helping network ministry on the basis of evaluation outcomes, changes or additions in service agencies, service agency personnel and contact numbers, and the production of new resource materials.

Identifying Agencies in the Public Domain

The soul community helps elders and their family members benefit from service providers in the public domain when they know who they are, what services they provide, and how to access the services. In this section, we will become acquainted with several agencies and programs that are essential parts of a helping network.

The Aging Network

As the result of the Older Americans Act (OAA) passed by Congress in 1965, the federal government, through the Administration on Aging, has provided funding to provider agencies at the local level. Over the years, these provider agencies have offered programs, services, and activities for elderly citizens. Social services, senior centers, and nutrition services such as congregate meals and home-delivered meals are examples of these offerings.

The OAA has gone through a number of amendments since 1965. However, important programs vital to the well-being of elders have continued and will not likely disappear. An aging network and a cadre of service professionals have evolved as a consequence of the OAA. This network has grown to include the whole array of local organizations and agencies that actually provide services to elders. We may learn about the aging network in a particular area by contacting the Area Agency on Aging (AAA) that plans, coordinates, and monitors locally oriented programs.

State Units on Aging

Every state has a comprehensive and coordinated system of agencies and organizations designed to meet the needs of its elder citizens. This system includes Planning and Service Areas (PSAs) that are served by AAAs. The AAAs administer programs and maintain subcontracts to service providers at the local level. Their intent is to respond to the needs of elders, their families, elected officials, and service provider agencies.

The AAAs are pivotal as information and referral (I&R) service providers. They give information about the availability of and access to services such as the following:

- Adult day health services
- Home health and personal care services
- Health screening
- Homemaker and home management services
- Alternate-living services
- Alzheimer's family support services
- Service plan assessment
- Assisted transportation
- Service case management
- Chore services
- Congregate meal sites and home-delivered meal services
- Continuing education opportunities
- Senior centers
- Elder abuse prevention information
- Emergency response systems
- Employment and job training
- Friendly visiting services
- Telephone assurance
- Shopping assistance
- Legal services and information
- Volunteer programs such as Foster Grandparents

Churches may obtain information about the Area Agency on Aging that serves their area and how to access it by contacting the state Department of Human Resource Services or the governor's office. Make these same contacts if changes occur in the way government agencies oversee aging services. Use the list and the self-test at the end of this chapter as guides to discover the locations and contact persons for helping agencies, programs, and services.

The Social Security Administration

People ask relatives, friends, and church leaders what to do and where to go to obtain retirement benefits (or information about them) through the Social Security Administration (SSA). But often they do not receive adequate information about the process, rules, payment, schedules, and eligibility for the various programs administered by this agency. Moreover, older people often need assistance in making telephone contact and in responding to application requests for detailed information.

The church as a soul community can be helpful to elders and family members by offering space for community forums on Social Security led by SSA staff. The soul community can also be helpful by giving out the national toll-free number for the Social Security Administration: (800) 772–1213. Individuals may call this number to obtain a Social Security card, a record of their earnings, an estimate of future Social Security benefits, and proof of payments received for Social Security (SS) or Supplemental Security Income (SSI) or both.

Individuals may also request an application for SS or SSI benefits through the toll-free number. However, because it is a mechanized number, callers must be prepared to remain on the line, to follow the prompting, and to refrain from getting discouraged. Local SSA offices may also be accessed for information and problem solving. Churches should also keep the numbers of these local offices on file.

Medicare and Medicaid

As in the case with Social Security, people often first seek information about signing up for Medicare and Medicaid from relatives, friends, and church leaders they think can help them. But they may not receive necessary information about the specific requirements and provisions of the programs. Churches should point out that the same toll-free number for Social Security may be used to obtain information about Medicare and Medicaid.

Housing and Related Assistance Programs

Older African Americans who do not have adequate financial resources can benefit from assistance in home maintenance costs and utilities. They will not always ask for this kind of assistance. However, church leaders can recognize the need through regular home visits to elders. They may also be apprised of concerns from family members, who themselves may not be able to help because of their own economic situations. An important role of the soul community is to be able to provide information about programs, home maintenance subsidies, and special utility rates for elders. The church's role may extend to helping elders and family members make contact with federal, regional, or local housing authorities and utility companies for information about assistance programs. Contact numbers for these agencies should be part of the helping network file.

Elders who experience decreases in their abilities to move about physically can also benefit from special housing. Again, church leaders can become cognizant of these conditions through regular visits to the homes of elders and through contacts with their relatives. An important role of the soul community is to advocate for living environments that respond to the needs of elders. The advocacy role can be carried out by helping elders and family members make contact with federal and local housing authorities for programs and subsidies designed for persons with difficult physical mobility problems.

Special programs offered through the U.S. Department of Housing and Urban Development include the Homeowner Rehabilitation Loan Program, rental assistance programs, and public housing programs. The Homeowner Rehabilitation Loan Program provides loans to qualified applicants for needed home repairs. Churches may obtain and maintain information on this program to share with elders and family members by contacting local city government planning offices. Rental assistance programs provide rent subsidies to low-income persons of all ages. Churches may obtain and maintain information on both rental assistance and public housing programs by contacting state or regional housing authorities. As in other instances, it is helpful for churches to provide the telephone numbers for these agencies.

Additional Helpers

Although not routinely considered part of the aging network, several other organizations routinely offer information, resource materials, services, and speakers on a variety of topics of interest to elders and their caregivers. These organizations include the following:

- The Alzheimer's Association. The information-only toll-free number is (800) 272–3900.
- The American Association of Retired Persons (AARP). Membership is open to persons aged fifty and over. The national toll-free number is (800) 424–3410, or phone a local AARP chapter.

- The National Council on Aging (NCOA). Make contact using the Washington, D.C., number (202) 479–1200, or the address at 600 Maryland Avenue, Washington, DC 20024.

- The Parish Nurse Resource Center. Phone (800) 556–5368 or write to 205 West Toughy Avenue, Suite 104, Park Ridge, IL 60068.

- Prison Fellowship USA. Phone (703) 478–0100 or write to the national headquarters for local prison ministry offices at P.O. Box 17500, Washington, DC 20041.

- National Association of People with AIDS. 1413 K Street NW, Washington, DC 20005. Phone (202) 898–0414.

- AIDS National Interfaith Network. Phone (800) 288–9619.

A more comprehensive list of agencies appears in the Questions for Reflection at the end of this chapter.

The Soul Community as a Helper Among Helpers

The soul community takes on an important role as it seeks to expand the pool of helpers that elders need for their well-being by linking with agencies in the public domain. It also plays a vital role as a helper among helpers through its ever-increasing effectiveness in directly addressing the real needs of elders and their families (Nichols, 1987). Chapter Seven highlighted types of initiatives churches can undertake as they seek to be soul communities and introduced two churches that had implemented activities. The following are outreach activities that many churches have sponsored and funded (Billingsley, 1992):

- Senior citizen housing to provide a safe and affordable living environment.

- Senior citizen centers and programs intended to provide social, educational, cultural, creative, spiritual, and recreational activities and trips. Programs also include transportation assistance, counseling, and hot meals.

- Food cooperatives designed to offer low-cost food, encourage good nutrition, and deliver food to families in need.

- Visitation ministries set up to give social, emotional, and spiritual support to elders through systematic visitations to those who are homebound, in nursing homes, or in prison.

Concluding Commentary

In this chapter, we discovered that the soul community can help expand the pool of helpers for elders and their families by building a helping network. We help in building this network through systematic approaches to identifying and connecting with service agencies in the public domain. The soul community also exists as a helper among helpers. The community carries out this role through self-funded outreach programs that directly address the needs of elders and their family helpers.

Questions for Reflection

1. Check off each agency about which you know the name, the services it provides, and its location:

    Administration on Aging (AOA)

    Your state unit on aging

    Your Area Agency on Aging (AAA)

    The Social Security office nearest you

    Medicare and Medicaid carrier

    Your private insurance carrier

    At least two suitable nursing homes in your area where family and friends can visit conveniently

    At least two personal care homes in your region

    At least two senior centers in your region

    The nearest hospital

    The nearest Veterans Administration (VA) hospital

    The nearest rural health clinic (if you live in a rural area)

    The nearest home health agency

    A Medicaid and non-Medicaid assisted transport company

    The Housing and Urban Development office and public housing authority

    The Equal Employment Opportunities Commission (EEOC)

    The Office of Consumer Affairs

    Alzheimer's Association chapter

    American Association of Retired Persons (AARP) chapter

National Council on Aging (NCOA)

U.S. Department of Family and Children's Services

2. Check off each program about which you know the name, the services it provides, and how to contact it:

The Food Stamp program

A home-delivered meals program

Elderly Legal Assistance Program (ELAP)

Homeowner Rehabilitation Loan Program

Rental assistance programs and public housing

Senior Community Services Employment Program (Title V)

Adult education or literacy programs

Senior discount programs

Low-income energy assistance program

Eldercare locator program

Utility budget programs

Support groups

9

PASTORAL CARE
AND NURTURE IN THE
SOUL COMMUNITY

Edward P. Wimberly

SISTER J WAS SEVENTY-EIGHT years old and had not attended church regularly ever since she began taking care of eighty-two-year-old Brother J after his stroke. Before this happened, she had taken joy in directing the children's choir. She was a superb musician and had been a public school music teacher.

Throughout the difficult period following Brother J's stroke, the pastor and members made numerous visits. They spent time just being with the couple, listening to them share their concerns, and doing what they could for them.

Brother J had another serious stroke and died. Sister J called the pastor, who went to her home to help with the funeral arrangements and to give spiritual support. Before going, the pastor, in turn, called the women's aid society and the current director of the children's choir.

Members of the society called a special meeting after they heard that Sister J was in trouble due to her husband's death. The women in the group knew that Sister J lived alone. They also knew that her daughter, who lived across town, would have her hands full helping her mother make arrangements and taking care of other family members upon their arrival from various parts of the country.

The women's society met to organize the activities they were accustomed to carrying out in such cases. They met to get things ready to care for Sister J and her family. The society decided who would make the phone call to Sister J to express the group's sympathy, to ask what she needed immediately, and to seek a time for visitors from the visitors' subcommittee to be with her. The hospitality sub-committee also made arrangements for food to take to the family and began working on preparations for food needed in the fellow-ship hall after the funeral.

The current director of the children's choir contacted the parents of the children. Through conversations with the parents and with the children, the choir decided to send original sympathy cards made by the children. They also decided to make a tape of one of Sister J's favorite songs she had taught them with a message on it from them. Their intent was to send it to her just to let her know they loved her.

The society was well prepared to take on its activities. It had a long tradition of doing that. The pastor of the congregation had also been very intentional about holding workshops and meeting with church auxiliaries on the whole matter of being a caring congregation.

--------- o ---------

The African American pastor and the women's aid society in this opening story were operating out of a long-established tradition in the African and African American community of honoring elders and caring for persons during dying and bereavement (Wimberly, 1976). Honoring elders in this tradition means supporting and car-ing for them and their families in times of crisis. As an activity, hon-oring is undertaken by clergy and laity alike. The clergy are the leaders who underscore the necessity of honoring in this way and do so themselves. The laity make up the natural helping group whose skills in giving support and care have often developed naturally. But focused attention still needs to be given to their ongoing develop-ment and the coordination of efforts so that attention to the well-being of the elders is always appropriately handled.

Our purpose in this chapter is to focus on what we do to honor the elders through pastoral care and nurture. Our concern will be for how we may use the natural helping structures of our churches to carry on the supporting and caring tasks that shape pastoral care. We will also focus on how our congregations can prepare for the supporting and caring tasks that define nurture.

Pastoral Care as an Honoring Initiative

When we engage in honoring elders through pastoral care, we place ourselves in close relationship with them and their family members. We become present with them, claiming our identity as a soul community. We recognize that doing so, in fact, denies the prevailing societal norm that emphasizes the detached individual, self-sufficient and self-regulated without thought of others (Oden, 1992).

Instead of acting on the prevailing societal norm, we focus on the value of human beings and the significance of communal values. We claim the long tradition of our church as an extended family, described by Anne Wimberly and Temba Mafico in Part One of this book. We embrace a worldview that emphasizes the vitality of the church as soul community resulting from caring and supportive relationships. And we claim this worldview as part of the soul theology that helps African Americans visualize ourselves as a soul community. In this way, we affirm the African proverb "I am because we are, and we are because I am."

Aspects of the Honoring Initiative

In the context of pastoral care, honoring takes the elders' overall needs seriously. Through pastoral care, we make sure that these needs are met. These holistic needs include their physical, emotional, interpersonal, spiritual, safety, social, and economic needs. In the case study, the women's aid society endeavored to meet the needs of Sister J and her family through phone calls, visitation, food, and other supports as identified by Sister J. The pastor also sought to respond to the family's needs through assistance in the funeral arrangements, prayers, and mobilizing the congregation's resources.

Pastoral Care and Cross-Generational Relationships

Within the ethos of the soul community, cross-generational relationships are essential for the survival of the individual and the whole community. This suggests to us an important role of cross-generational pastoral care to provide meaning in the lives of elders and to sustain them in times of crisis. In the opening story, the director of the children's choir, the children's parents, and the children themselves found creative ways of giving pastoral care to Sister J.

The effort of the children's choir shows that we can be quite creative in the compassionate caring we give to elders. And as told in Chapter Three, compassionate caring is a way of "stepping into the shoes of the elders," allowing ourselves to see their situations.

Pastoral Care and Life Cycle Stages

Honoring initiatives through pastoral care should also recognize the different stages of the older adult life cycle. For example, it is important for us to distinguish between an older adult who is capable of full involvement in the community, those who need limited involvement, and those who need to be cared for due to declining physical and mental capacities. In our honoring of elders, we must make sure that they maintain a level of well-being and involvement that reflects their existing capabilities and interests.

In our honoring, we must take care not to exclude elders from community activities. We care for them by keeping them connected as long as possible with activities that have meaning for them. This means that we value the role of the elder as steward of the treasures of wisdom and values that can only be passed on through vital relationships (Wimberly, 1982). Stewards are not disciples in the sense of being groomed in the tradition; rather, stewards are custodians who are charged with the responsibility of upholding the community's values and making sure that they are transmitted to future generations. This transmitting comes through relationships and cross-generational connections.

Pastoral Care and Life Situations

Honoring elders through pastoral care takes seriously specific life situations that elders must negotiate. As long as elders can care for themselves and live independently, pastoral care responds to elders as active participating members of the community. However, when an elder loses some abilities to live wholly independently, pastoral care involves making sure that the elder's needs are met by the caring community.

Also, regardless of age, every elder has certain life tasks to perform. These tasks are associated with the elder's movement through the later years and include affirming a positive self-identity despite the many changes and losses they face, including retirement, loss of income, loss of loved ones, and health problems.

Moreover, the task of elders is to maintain a sense of meaning and purpose in life that often requires knowing that they are needed in some way. Of significance is the elders' need to feel that they are making a contribution to the next generation. For African American elders, this has often meant having significant extended family relationships with younger generations. Insofar as we take seriously these tasks and afford opportunities for elders to tell how the community can be helpful to them in addressing the tasks, we honor them.

Pastoral Care and the Larger Society

Honoring African American elders through pastoral care initiatives intentionally considers the larger society in which African American elders exist. This means being aware of a societal ethos that is youth-oriented and tends to be denigrating not only of the elders' age but also of their ethnicity. We also recognize that many elders depend solely on Social Security, have restrictive health benefits, experience housing difficulties, and recall assaults to their selfhood resulting from racial discrimination and racism.

The significance of these issues for pastoral care is that they affect the elders' well-being. Consequently, they cannot be ignored. The role of pastoral care is to discover ways of addressing these issues, including the provision of needed resources and activities as outlined in the preceding chapters.

Pastoral Care Through Storytelling and Listening

There is something therapeutic about telling our story. When we tell it to someone, we feel ourselves connected by their being with us in the telling and by their listening to us. When we tell our story, we affirm ourselves as living a full life, with all its joys, sorrows, challenges, and possibilities. When we tell our story, we unburden ourselves. We let go of the things that trouble us. And when a compassionate other hears us and responds to us with care, we feel sustained, even if our situation causing the trouble does not demonstrably change.

This is no less the case with elders. Elders need and want opportunities to tell their stories, and they want to tell them to others who will listen compassionately. Offering these opportunities and the listening presence are part of what we do in pastoral care. We honor the elders in this way.

Indeed, storytelling and listening have become the basis for pastoral care and of Christian education as nurture within the African

American church. Anne Streaty Wimberly has developed storytelling and listening as a caring and teaching strategy in *Soul Stories: African American Christian Education* (1994b), and I have analyzed the implications of storytelling and listening for the care of persons in *African American Pastoral Care* (E. P. Wimberly, 1991).

An important way in which we incorporate storytelling and listening into what we do to care for elders is to invite them to draw on their own life stories and Bible stories that are similar to the circumstances of their lives. In this way, we help them tap into faith tradition found in Scripture for what it has to say for their lives in good times and in times of crisis. This also takes into consideration the interest in Bible study and prayer many African American elders have. And it supports and guides this activity, along with prayer, as means of spiritual self-care.

We also honor the elders through storytelling and listening activities because we accept that elders are the custodians of the treasured values and worldview. And they can transmit this worldview through a storytelling and listening modality.

Revisiting Pastoral Care and the Holistic Needs of Elders

We stated earlier that honoring elders through pastoral care takes their holistic needs seriously. In this section, our intent is to focus on specific levels of pastoral care that respond to these needs.

Pastoral care for addressing the holistic needs of African American elders must be provided on several levels. The first level responds to the immediate needs of the elders by providing a therapeutic relationship and a caring environment. The second level is making sure that the social context in which the elders live is a responsive one. The third level of pastoral care moves into the area of nurture, where the caring community is trained to respond to the elders' needs.

Confronting obstacles in achieving life goals that cannot be surmounted immediately by ordinary problem-solving means places elders in a crisis situation (Wimberly, 1976). Examples of life goals include moving from one stage of the life cycle to another and achieving emotional, interpersonal, physical, and spiritual well-being. Losses of any kind are potential threats to life goals. Lack of financial support and limited housing, income, and medical attention are threats to the well-being of elders. These concerns need to be addressed.

The first line of offense for pastoral care to African American elders in crisis is to intervene in a caring and facilitative way to shore up their ability to cope with the crisis. The first task is to help people understand what is happening to them. During crises, elders' thinking is disorganized and confused, and they need help in organizing their thoughts and behavior.

Once the person has some degree of control over the crisis, the caregiver must mobilize the caring community to assist in the person's crisis adjustment. The dying man had a lot of unfinished business with family members that needed immediate attention. Therefore, the pastor made sure that family members and selected members of the congregation began to reach out to the dying man. The goal was to give him support during the last days of his life.

The second level of pastoral care deals with the wider social context. Its goal is to make sure that the person has the physical, interpersonal, and psychosocial resources needed to meet the crisis at hand. Physical resources are supplies necessary to satisfy basic biological needs, including food, shelter, sensory stimulation, health and medical care, and exercise opportunities. Someone must see to it that these basic physical needs are met so that the elderly can take full advantage of their growth opportunities. The government provides Social Security, Medicare, and Medicaid for the basic needs of persons, but these resources are often insufficient. Many African American elders have no way to supplement this income and therefore often need assistance in finding adequate resources. At this level, pastoral care involves making sure that resources exist to ensure the basic supplies of elders. This may mean doing political lobbying for specific bills, community organizing for specific tasks related to the elderly, and forming groups in the church and the larger community to see that certain things get done. This phase also involves influencing policymaking so that elders' needs are adequately understood and responded to by social and political institutions.

Interpersonal and psychosocial resources relate to the elders' needs for close relationships and interaction with family, friends, peers, and the community. Humans never lose their need for love, affection, participation, and group activity. The black church has been excellent in providing for these psychosocial needs, but there are dangers that threaten what the black church has historically been able to do. One such threat is the overemphasis on youth to the neglect of the needs for the elders in wider society, and another is the emphasis on self-sufficiency and autonomy whereby people are expected to "go it alone" in this society. Such emphases are lethal when they threaten elders' participation in community life. Some evidence exists that these orientations can erode the cross-generational and communal emphases of historic black churches. Consequently, pastoral care must continually address assumptions that undergird the caring activity of the church and make sure that the caring practice is based on sound assumptions.

The third level of pastoral care involves training the congregation for its role in pastoral care. This has to do with the nurture of congregants.

Nurture in Pastoral Care

As indicated earlier, nurture is the preparation of the congregation for its role in developing a caring community and support structures for elders (Wimberly and Wimberly, 1995). In other words, nurture is teaching people how to play their roles in the soul community. A critical task of nurture is to create caring environments in the church and supportive networks by enabling life review and storytelling as basic healing dimensions for elders. Life review involves recalling and elucidating earlier experiences in life to bring added meaning and perspective to the present. The process also involves telling important stories from early life. Life review and storytelling require time, and others must recognize this need as a normal part of the aging process as well as an instructive activity for everyone. Consequently, families and church members must be trained to recognize this need when planning ways for elders to participate in the community.

Congregants and families also need to be aware of the many negative stereotypes about the elderly and how they influence actual caring for elders. One stereotype is that elders should be set aside because they are no longer useful. Another is that elders should become inactive when they reach retirement age. Such negative myths make it difficult for elders to become or remain involved in meaningful activities that could benefit and enrich the life of the entire church and community. The educational ministry has to address and dispel these stereotypes.

The congregation also has to be trained in the meaning, functions, and principles of support systems. Support systems help people maintain physical, emotional, and spiritual integrity, and church members must be made aware that they form support systems for elders. Therefore, they need to know about building and sustaining relationships with elders, the different phases of elderhood, and the physical, interpersonal, and psychosocial needs of the elderly. They need to develop skills for including elders in activities that the elders enjoy and feel comfortable doing.

First and foremost, congregants must understand the needs of elders and that these needs are varied. For example, elders have recreational needs, leisure needs, learning needs, needs for involvement and participation in church and community life, needs related to acquiring specific skills (such as reading, writing, and computer use), needs to engage in activities that benefit others, and needs to learn skills that help them maintain some measure of control over their lives as they grow older (Wimberly, 1981). They also need activities related to continued self-development and spiritual needs.

The needs of elders for activity and involvement in the life of the church and the community vary, depending on whether an elder is one of the young old, middle old, or later old (Wimberly, 1981). For the young old, ages fifty through sixty-nine, needs relate to planning for later years, rediscovering physical abilities, and discovering new interests and activities. In middle old age, or ages seventy through eighty-four, activity and involvement needs relate to personal dignity, control of one's environment, satisfaction obtained through fewer or less strenuous activities, continuing to make contributions to others, and continued interaction with multiple generations. In later old age, ages eighty-five and older, the concerns are staying independent as long as possible and continuing to be engaged in meaningful activities as long as possible based on physical and mental capacities. Awareness of these needs is important when preparing persons for their role in creating a supportive environment of elder participation.

In training congregants for their role in developing a caring environment for African American elders, there is a need to explore stereotypes about the aging process. Some of these stereotypes are that aging is accompanied by disabling diseases, dependence, unattractiveness, impoverishment, loneliness, inflexibility, depression, and childishness. The reality is that the majority of elders are healthy and as functional as they choose to be, and experience varying degrees of physical, mental, and social disability. It is not possible to put all aging persons into a single stereotypical category. Often elders are devalued and treated as second-class citizens. Such inappropriate attitudes must be attended to early in the training process.

Of specific importance is for congregants to create storytelling environments for elders to enrich their own lives and the lives of others. There are specific things that can be taught for creating storytelling environments.

The first thing is to enable a storytelling environment where elders can do life review through storytelling. The significance of life review is that it gives significant meaning to the life of the elder, helps the elder deal with fears of growing old, provides comfort during difficult times, and helps provide a sense of closure in preparation for death. Life review is an adaptive as well as a creative process that is basic to aging. Moreover, important intellectual processes that draw on experience and accumulated informal learning increase as one grows older, and life review aids in these processes. Consequently, persons who seek to keep elders involved in community life have to be aware of the intellectual and creative thought processes that go on in life review.

The best way to prepare congregants for assisting elders in life review and storytelling is to create a storytelling environment. This involves establishing a setting in which stories are shared all the time. Creating such an environment involves "story linking," helping persons reflect on their everyday lives and issues in light of stories from their faith communities (Wimberly, 1994b). The goal of story linking is to help persons see the unfolding of their personal lives in light of the wider story of the Christian faith and the related faith stories that come from the African American community. Persons young and old need to envisage their lives in light of its relationship to a larger story. The elderly also have this need to be continually reminded that their lives are meaningful and purposeful as part of a larger unfolding story that is moving toward a particular goal.

The methods of story linking include enabling people to tell their own stories, helping them learn Bible stories and stories from the faith tradition and African American tradition, bringing their own stories in line with those of the faith community and Scripture, and learning to orient and make decisions in light of reflection on these stories. Those responsible for involving elders in the community must learn the different phases and methods of story linking so as to facilitate this activity with elders.

Concluding Commentary

This chapter presented ways to do pastoral care and nurture with African American elders. Pastoral care has focused on bringing to bear on the holistic needs of elders all the resources of church and community. The worldview undergirding care, life cycle concerns and tasks, cross-generational relationships, and storytelling and listening were emphasized. Nurture was defined as preparing the entire congregation for its role in responding to the holistic needs of the elderly. The mobilization of the soul community as a support system for elders was highlighted as an essential aspect of pastoral care.

Questions for Reflection

1. Name some of the elders in your church that come to mind. What kinds of needs do they have? List these needs, and try to be as inclusive of each elder as a whole person—that is, include emotional, interpersonal, psychosocial, physical, spiritual, material, financial, and other needs.

2. Think about persons who are aged fifty-five to sixty-nine, seventy to eighty-four, and eighty-five and older. How do their needs differ? How are they the same? How has your church kept the elders involved in the life of the church? How do you feel about the record of your church in involving elders in the total life of the church?

3. List some of the stereotypes that you have heard about elders. How accurate or inaccurate are they?

4. List some of the ways in which the church can be a support system for persons in the different older adult age groups. How could your church be more responsive to the pastoral care and nurture needs of persons in these age groups in your congregation?

10

HEALTH, ILLNESS, AND DEATH IN THE CONTEXT OF THE SOUL COMMUNITY

Anne Streaty Wimberly

MR. AND MRS. M HAD EXPERIENCED moderately good health for a number of years after their retirement, with the exception of Mrs. M's continuing battle with hypertension. They were an active couple who enjoyed independent living, involvement in church and family life, and "good eating," as Mrs. M put it. But after hospitalization for dangerously high blood pressure, mental confusion, and pneumonia, Mrs. M, who at the time was in her early eighties, experienced rapidly declining health. Responsibility for Mrs. M's care upon her release from the hospital became overwhelming for Mr. M, who was in his mid-eighties. But both Mr. and Mrs. M were adamant about staying in their own home. They had also said many times to their adult children, who lived in another state, that they never wanted to be "put away" in a nursing home. The children promised that they would honor their parents' wishes. But they were also unprepared for what was happening to their parents.

Members of Mr. and Mrs. M's church and their neighbors helped them when they could. The couple's children called constantly and made frequent visits. Other relatives living in the area could not help because they themselves were elderly and in need of care. Mrs.

M's health continued to deteriorate. Her doctor recommended in-home caregivers to provide health and homemaking support so that the couple could stay in their home, and the couple and their children agreed.

After a short period of in-home care, the caregiver called the children to indicate that Mrs. M had fallen several times and had to be transported to the hospital. Mrs. M's physician told the children upon their arrival that although Mrs. M had no broken bones, there was clear concern for her future safety and well-being. Also, Mr. M had become depressed, was not eating properly, and was sleeping much of the time. His health had also become a concern. The physician strongly advised the children to make arrangements to remove their parents from their home and place them in a safe environment. Mr. and Mrs. M remained adamant about staying in their home. The children did not want to take away their parents' right to decide, but they knew something needed to be done. After lengthy and difficult discussions, the parents agreed to rent out their home and move in with one of their children.

Mr. and Mrs. M's adjustment to their loss of independent living was not easy. The family also had to make big adjustments. Over time, Mr. M found new activities and made new friends in a senior center. His health improved. Mrs. M suffered a series of strokes and became semicomatose. The attending physician at the hospital asked Mrs. M's husband and her adult child, who had power of attorney, to decide if they wished to sign a living will on Mrs. M's behalf. They agreed with everything except the withdrawal of forced feeding. The seriousness of Mrs. M's health and impending death also prompted Mr. M to talk about the kinds of arrangements he would want for himself and Mrs. M upon their death. He wanted both to be returned to their hometown. In the meantime, the family's decision was to keep both parents in their home with the assistance of medical supports and in-home caregivers.

○

This case study reveals the nature of some of the difficult issues and decisions this African American family faced. But the story of Mr. and Mrs. M and their adult children is not unusual, given the realities of wellness, illness, and death among American elders. In this chapter, we will consider these realities and concrete ways the soul community may honor elders by showing compassion in matters of wellness, illness, and death.

Realities of Health Problems Among African American Elders

In the opening story, we found that Mrs. M had ongoing problems with hypertension. She was later hospitalized for it and experienced disabling consequences from it. She also had other health problems. The reality is that people in every ethnic group generally experience more problems with their physical health as they age. However, compared to other Americans, African American elders experience greater rates of disabling conditions and limitations in activities, due mostly to chronic conditions. They have higher rates of illness and death.

Census Bureau data show that persons born in 1991 have an overall life expectancy of 75.5 years. African Americans born in that year have a life expectancy of slightly more than seventy years. But the life expectancy of African American males is sixty-five years. Yet African Americans who reach age seventy-five tend to live a great deal longer (Jackson, 1988; Manuel, 1988; American Society on Aging, 1992).

Risk Factors for Disease

Risk factors are predisposing conditions that lead to illness. Prevalent risk factors for disease in African Americans include high serum cholesterol levels, poor diet, obesity, lack of exercise, stress, and smoking. These risk factors contribute greatly to the high incidence of heart disease among us. Moreover, smoking, poor diet, and alcohol contribute to the high incidence of certain cancers among us. In fact, cancer is the second leading cause of death among African Americans. In addition, poor diet, obesity, alcohol, and lack of exercise are factors in diabetes, which is the third leading cause of death among us (American Association of Retired Persons, 1991). Most of all, these diseases are preventable or manageable.

Alzheimer's is a dementing disease that is receiving continuing attention. Though its prevalence rates in African American elders is not known, it does exist. However, in his review of illnesses that cause cognitive impairment, Baker (1988) indicates that African Americans show increased risk for the dementing consequences of stroke due to hypertension and alcoholic dementia due to alcohol misuse, abuse, or dependence.

These risk factors for disease cause problems in our older years when such factors are ignored. This means that gaining knowledge of and responding to the risk factors is an important responsibility for elders and family members alike. It is the responsibility of the entire soul community.

Mrs. M experienced high blood pressure, known as hypertension. Roughly one-third of African Americans have hypertension, and its prevalence increases with age. And African American women aged sixty-five and over are at greater risk for it than any other group in the United States. Hypertension is regarded as the most serious threat to our health because of its devastating impact on the cardiovascular and cerebrovascular system. Heart disease is the leading cause of death among us, but as a group, we also experience high incidence of stroke, kidney disease, and kidney failure, all related to hypertension (Anderson, 1988; Curry, 1990; American Association of Retired Persons, 1993a). An often unmentioned reality as well is that the number of older people who are being infected with HIV/AIDS is rising among both men and women. Moreover, some grandparents are raising grandchildren who have been orphaned by AIDS. AIDS is a multigenerational issue. Elders in particular face special problems of greater risk of misdiagnosis, discrimination, social isolation, lack of caregivers, and cost of care (American Association of Retired Persons, 1996).

Promoting Health Through Self-Care and Family Care

Promoting health through self-care for older adults is gaining recognition in the formal health care system as a means of improving health outcomes and helping elders live satisfying lives (Mockenhaupt, 1993). An entire 1993 issue of *Generations,* the Journal of the American Society on Aging, emphasized it.

Much is also being said about health promotion in churches. Parish nurse programs are being developed by churches that focus not only on health through self-care but also on the role of the whole family in promoting the health of every member. These initiatives are being supported by efforts of the National Parish Resource Center, located in Park Ridge, Illinois. Identified in Chapter Eight, this agency provides resources on the role of parish nurse professionals and services that promote health and wellness within the church community.

One example of a parish nurse program is taking place in Atlanta, Georgia, through St. Joseph's Hospital. The hospital trains nurses to work through the churches who hire them. The churches refer persons needing care to the nurses. A part of the nurses' responsibility is to make home visits and provide treatment. Another pivotal aspect is health education. But the significance of the parish nurse program lies in the responsibility the church assumes for the health of its members. It is the responsibility of the church as family.

Our churches' role in health promotion is a pivotal one because they are institutions to which elders as well as family and friends belong. As such, we have an opportunity to reach elders and others in a way that formal institutions have not been able to do to any appreciable extent.

Our churches' promotion of health through self-care and family care is important for several reasons. First, an emphasis on both self and family draws attention to what elders and the whole congregation can do to maintain health and cope with illness. This approach also highlights that the status of our health in our elder years is often a consequence of the extent of care given to our health in prior years. Second, a self and family approach stresses the idea that what happens to one person happens to another and what happens to one person has consequences for others' lives. Through this approach, then, elders can be resourceful participants on their own behalf and enter into resourceful participation with others. It is a communal approach that shows our sense of peoplehood and solidarity, which defines our church as a soul community.

Finally, when we develop programs that give attention to health, we take seriously the older adult ministry goal of well-being, which was proposed in Chapter Four. And when we emphasize the importance of health promotion and help elders and others develop requisite skills, we are really accentuating what it means to demonstrate true respect for self and others. We honor both elders and ourselves.

Accomplishing this initiative can be a challenging pursuit, however. It is challenging because actively promoting health through self-care and family care requires that we first recognize the health situations of elders and the threats to other members' health. Second, it requires us to insist unequivocally that the church is an appropriate place to promote it. Third, it requires us to engage in moral discourse. That is, it requires us intentionally to provide a safe space for people to explore together obstacles to health, their commitments to act wisely in health matters, and to consider how to deal with illness. Finally, it requires us to be compassionate carers.

As noted in Chapter Three, we show compassion when we listen, affirm, and comfort. But we also aggressively pursue the truth about actions that promote health and actively engage the elders and others in this pursuit. Compassionate carers, then, must at times be compassionate challengers who work for a balance between giving tough messages and allowing persons to deal with the tough realities of their lives. It requires methods that move people toward voluntarily changing health-negating behaviors to those that promote health.

Key Actions in Health Promotion

Compassionate challengers make people aware of actions that are crucial to the promotion of wellness in the elder years as well as the years leading up to them. Of particular importance in the African American community are actions that help persons adopt and maintain good dietary habits, work on stress reduction, engage in helpful exercise, and seek ongoing medical oversight.

DIETARY HABITS. Dietary habits underlie nearly all of the risk factors already mentioned, and good eating habits can prevent or control disease. Yet these habits are among the most difficult to maintain. The American Association of Retired Persons (AARP) and the Administration on Aging conducted a study of six African American focus groups, aimed at identifying African American health-related practices, behaviors, and attitudes. The focus groups consisted of elders, mostly low-income, residing in the cities of Washington, Detroit, and Memphis. The study found that the elders knew that health maintenance includes eating proper foods. However, many of them reported that they do not regularly do so (Henderson, Kensinger, and RIVA, 1992).

In fact, it is common in our homes, at church suppers, and at other social events for meals to include fatty fried meats, foods highly salted and prepared with animal fats or lard, and desserts high in sugar and fat. It is equally common for elders and family members to resist changes in eating habits because, as one elder remarked, "What you're asking is for me to take the joy out of eating." In the opening story, Mrs. M spoke of the importance of "good eating."

The story of another elder also reveals additional reasons for not making needed changes in dietary habits: Mrs. X's limited resources cause her to cut corners to make ends meet. As a result, she eats poorly. Her diet consists mainly of carbohydrate and fat. She admits to having a sweet tooth and to snacking between meals. She is aware of her body size (obese) but states that she finds it hard to act differently. Mrs. X indicated that when her husband was alive, she took pleasure in preparing special dishes because she knew there was someone with whom to share them and from whom she would receive appreciation. Now, she says, she is not inclined to do anything—not even prepare herself three meals a day. Instead, Mrs. X eats anything that is easy to prepare and that she finds "filling" (Boykin-Barringer, 1990).

These responses of elders highlight the complexity of people's willingness and ability to address the matter of diet forthrightly. Nonetheless, it is incumbent on the soul community to apprise people of good dietary habits because of what is at stake if it does not and because doing so honors God's value placed on us. Doing so honors God and elders; in fact, it honors the whole community.

Compassionate challenger strategies may include alerting the community about the necessity of good dietary habits through periodic "spotlight on health" announcements during community gatherings, distribution of dietary information, and church-sponsored workshops or notices about them in the community. The content of the strategies may be drawn from such resources as *Health Risks and Preventive Care Among Older Blacks* and *Nutrition for Black Older Adults: Healthy Tomorrows,* both published by the American Association of Retired Persons, 601 E Street, NW, Washington, DC 20049. Also, sponsor soul community meals to showcase tasty ethnic dishes that promote healthful eating. The meal could be based on a predetermined menu, or it could be a potluck with food prepared from health-wise recipes. Community members may share recipes.

EXERCISE. A second key finding in the six African American focus groups mentioned earlier was that the elders knew the importance of balancing good eating habits with exercise. However, as was the case with eating properly, many of them reported that they do not exercise regularly. The role of the compassionate challenger is an important one in summoning elders, and indeed the whole community, to more intentional care of self. The summons is based on the reality that "one of the major benefits of regular physical activity is protection against coronary heart disease. Physical activity also provides some protection against other chronic diseases such as adult-onset diabetes, arthritis, hypertension, certain cancers, osteoporosis and depression" (American Association of Retired Persons, 1995, p. 2).

Exercise builds muscle tone that helps strengthen the lungs and prevent falls and broken bones. In addition, research has proved that exercise can ease tension and reduce the amount of stress people experience. Simply stated, exercise is one of the best things elders and all others can do to promote wellness. It makes people feel good (American Association of Retired Persons, 1995; American Association of Retired Persons, 1991b).

Challenging elders to promote good health through exercise often requires the soul community's awareness of three main barriers that restrict or impede involvement in exercise. One of these barriers is inconvenient or unsafe locations for outside exercise such as walking. A second barrier is elders' lack of knowledge about kinds of exercise they might enjoy doing within health limitations. A third barrier is churches' lack of knowledge about fitness and exercise programs that they may sponsor. Two resources that may be used to address these barriers are published by the AARP:

> *Pep Up Your Life: A Fitness Book for Mid-Life and Older Persons.* This resource suggests exercises that can be undertaken at home, including in a wheelchair, as well as outside the home, including outdoors or in a mall. The exercises are organized in three endurance levels.
>
> *Staying Well: Health Promotion Programs for Older Persons.* This book presents a number of fitness and exercise programs especially designed for elders. It also tells how to access these programs or receive materials useful in the home or in church-sponsored initiatives.

Through the soul community's provision of helpful resources, getting information and making contact with programs, and sponsoring programs, it takes on the necessary role of compassionate advocate.

STRESS MANAGEMENT. In the opening story, Mr. M was overwhelmed by his wife's debilitating illness and the care she required upon release from the hospital. As a result, he became depressed, stopped eating properly, and began to sleep a lot. His physical health began to suffer. In another situation, an elderly woman became increasingly anxious because of limited finances. She was depressed, and she failed to get prescribed medicines. In still another case, an elderly widow, who lives alone in a difficult neighborhood, worried about her safety. She could not sleep at night. As a result, she failed to get the rest her doctor told her was essential to her health. And in

one case, an elderly widow suffered great stress because of unresolved differences between her and her daughter, to the extent that
her physical health was being compromised.

Elders undergo changes and experiences in their lives that sometimes cause stress. Whether of relational, economic, or psychological
origin, the stress elders feel is very real and can have consequences
for their health. As a result, the soul community that shows concern
for the wellness of elders envisions ways of assisting their process of
stress management. We have already learned that exercise promotes
physical and emotional health by easing tension and reducing stress.
However, it is important for the soul community to foster other approaches to stress management.

Studies have shown that African American elders tend to be effective
copers (Chatters and Taylor, 1989). However, often their primary coping approach is to rely on spiritual resources, such as prayer and Bible
study. This approach reflects, in part, their belief in an ever-present
and sustaining God. But it also derives, in part, from the difficulty of
some to find persons who have time and skills to be with them, listen
to them, and support their efforts to ease their anxiety. As an elderly
widow put it, "I have friends who call me all the time. But they're so
busy telling me about everything that's going on with them that I
rarely get a chance to say what's going on with me. I've been going
through a lot since my husband's death. But mostly I just hold it in or
take it to the Lord. It would be nice, though, if there was somebody
that I could really level with. I need that. It would really help."

This elder's words suggest that stress reduction may be aided
through relationships with others who, as stated in Chapter Three,
serve as a compassionate presence, as listeners and interpreters with
elders. The soul community makes compassion come alive through
its genuine interest in those who suffer. What specific strategy can
the soul community use to make this happen in honoring ways?

A key strategy entails the community's development of a ministry
focused, first, on compassionate presence with elders through intentional outreach to elders wherever they are—in their private resi-
dences in the community, in senior high-rises or apartments, in
personal care homes or nursing homes, or in hospitals. Compassionate presence through outreach takes the form of systematic in-person
visits and phone visits. A key way of implementing this strategy is
to organize an initiative called Caring Partners (a project originated
by the United Methodist Church in Evanston, Illinois, as the
African American Clergy and Spouse Retirement Transition

Project). It entails recruiting younger persons who agree to being paired with an elder who seeks such a partnership. The partners establish regular times to be together in person or to chat on the phone.

The second aspect of the strategy for implementation by partners is compassionate listening. Although open sharing through dialogue is encouraged between the partners, ample time must be given to the elder's story. The intent is to build a relational climate that allows elders to entrust their stories, including their anxieties and concerns, to another person without fear of its being misused or taken beyond the relationship. For this to happen, younger persons who establish partnerships with elders have to be prepared for effective listening. Prospective listeners must be made aware that listening is a difficult art when it is seriously employed. It requires that listeners be constantly aware on many levels, including these (Cedarleaf, 1984, 1990; Dass and Gorman, 1985; Howe, 1965):

- Their level of interest in listening
- Their ability to understand what they are hearing and to refrain from judging
- Their facility in refraining from anxious activity, such as nervous laughter, interrupting the flow of the elder's story, or ending the visit prematurely
- Their ability to refrain from letting personal worries disable listening to the elder or from focusing on their own thoughts in ways that prevent them from being with the elder
- Their awareness of their own fatigue that can impede their ability to listen
- Their ability to sense intuitively when to bring the time of sharing to a close

Preparing partners to be compassionate listeners also entails helping them see the difference between passive listening and active listening skills. In passive, or quiet, listening, the listening partner does not interrupt the flow of sharing. Emphasis is on the elder's talking through a personal story, worries, or fears and the listener's attentiveness by means of a glance or touch or, in phone listening, a word or sound that lets the elder know you are there and listening. Active listening entails the listener's caring and unobtrusive offering of quiet questions, comments, or sensitive stories (Cedarleaf, 1990).

The third part of the strategy of developing a ministry focused on compassionate presence with elders through caring partners involves the role of the partner as compassionate discernment guide. The compassionate discernment guide extends the skills used as a compassionate presence and listener. The purpose of the discernment guide is to help elders envision positive meanings and actions in their lives that offer them hope. Partners who serve as guides in the discernment process may share with elders what they understand as the elder's story, engage elders in reflecting on meanings they assign to what is happening or has happened to them that is causing anxiety, and invite them to think about how and from where relief and hope may come and what they may do to make it possible.

REGULAR HEALTH CHECKUPS. Study findings from the African American focus groups mentioned earlier also show that some elders seek regular medical attention and treatment when they first exhibit symptoms. However, others fail to do so until home remedies fail and their symptoms persist. Failure to seek help can result from lack of finances or little or no insurance coverage as well as from poor relations between the elders and health care providers (Henderson, Kensinger, and RIVA, 1992).

Given these realities, the soul community's roles of compassionate challenger and advocate can make a difference. This means that the community highlights the necessity of regular checkups as means of promoting wellness. The community finds out where health screenings are offered at nominal or no cost and searches for ways of contributing to the cost of regular checkups. The community arranges for transportation of elders to checkup sites.

Regular health checkups also include elders' involvement in twelve-step programs and support groups such as Alcoholics Anonymous, Narcotics Anonymous, and women's and men's issues support groups. The challenger and advocate roles of the soul community continue in these areas of health promotion. Encouraging elders' participation in groups of benefit to them, finding such groups, and sponsoring them are ways these roles may be activated.

Some Ideas for Getting Started in Health Promotion Ministry

Optimally, ideas designed to promote wellness among African American elders are also directed toward family members and the whole community. In this way, wellness becomes not only the concern of elders but also the responsibility of those moving toward elder-hood. Promoting wellness is a lifelong venture. It is a crucial part of ministry in the soul community. In recognizing this, the soul community honors not simply elders but also the stage of life called elder-hood. Here are some action ideas for getting started in health promotion ministries:

- *Develop a health and welfare ministries committee.* Form the committee to develop goals and strategies to promote elders' well-being. Include elders on the committee.

- *Organize health awareness groups.* Invite as speakers on various topics health professionals who are members or who are associated with local hospitals, schools, health maintenance organizations (HMOs), county extension services, or other agencies serving elders.

- *Offer health promotion seminars.* Use speakers, demonstrations, and audiovisual resources to communicate information on modifiable risk factors for HIV and AIDS and how to address them. Reward participants with "diplomas" or certificates.

- *Obtain and distribute health promotion materials.* Assign specific members of the health and welfare ministries committee responsibility for finding, obtaining, and distributing circulars, pamphlets, and resources that provide helpful information on health promotion and disease prevention.

A model for ministry that tends to all aspects of the well-being of African Americans, including elders, is found in the work of the Center for Holistic Ministry at Covenant Baptist Church in Washington, D.C. The center developed out of the church's belief that the African American church has considered itself God's change agent in times past, and it must function in the same manner today. And it must do so from the premise that ministries directed toward persons' well-being must be ministries focused on the whole person. Among the programmatic thrusts are health and nutrition, substance abuse treatment and prevention, support and special-interest groups, life skills, and economic empowerment (Wiley, 1991).

The Soul Community Response to Serious Illness

The opening story of Mr. and Mrs. M reminds us that illness changes the lives of elders experiencing it and family members who must decide on their care. Whether in cases of chronic illnesses, dementia caused by Alzheimer's disease, or other debilitating or terminal illnesses, families are often called on to decide where and how the elder will be cared for and to make appropriate arrangements. In other instances, family members become the caregivers for a seriously ill elder either in the elder's home or in their own.

The sick elder and family members must work through feelings about the physical condition, the possible death of the elder, and the nature of responsibilities they must undertake. Experiences of serious illness of elders are not easily handled. Every person involved needs support. To this extent, in times of serious illness, honoring elders requires support from the soul community. The church as a soul community is called to assure the dignity of elders and the caregivers through knowing the situations of family members and caregivers and giving support to elders and their families.

Know the Situations of Families

Support for both elders and family members is pivotal because the family represents the core group that has responsibility for the well-being of elders. Many patterns exist for establishing the place of family caregiving. African American elders who have already resided for a lengthy period with children or in extended family households receive assistance from family members in these contexts as long as the family can provide it. Elders living independently receive help first from spouses or relatives who live nearby. When necessary, relatives who live at a distance relocate temporarily to assist the elder. It is also common for relatives, near or distant, to move into their homes elders who have lived independently throughout their adult lives (Taylor, 1988).

African American families are typically reluctant to rely on nursing homes, personal care homes, or hospices to provide care for their elders. The cultural precept is to "care for your own." However, there are instances when the nursing home or some other long-stay institution provides a needed and more realistic caregiving alternative. On this basis, fewer than one in twenty African American elders enter long-stay institutions (Carter, 1988).

The most common experience, however, is for family members to provide long-term care for elders with severe, debilitating, or terminal illnesses in a family context. This experience typically includes assisting with personal care, mobility and activities of daily living, and nursing care, sometimes with help from professional health care providers.

Know the Impact of Family Caregiving and Ethical Dilemmas of Decision Making

Family members try to do the best they can to care for a severely ill elder. But caregiving can be demanding, disruptive, and expensive. Moreover, attempting to make decisions in the best interest of all concerned sometimes poses ethical dilemmas that people find hard to reconcile. The case of Mr. and Mrs. P reflect some of these troubling aspects of family caregiving and decision making.

After Mr. P had one leg amputated because of diabetes at age seventy-four, he was in the hospital for a long time. Mrs. P, aged seventy-one, visited him every day. She was ecstatic when she learned that he would soon be released. In preparation for her husband's return home, Mrs. P had wheelchair ramps built outside and inside. She learned how to assist him with bathing, toilet use, and other personal care tasks. She learned how to give insulin injections and to care for the site of his surgery. She collected recipes to ensure the proper diet for him.

But Mrs. P was not prepared for the seeming twenty-four-hour schedule of caregiving she undertook. She had no time to herself. She lost sleep because of care her husband needed and demanded throughout the night. She worried about the mounting medical bills not covered by insurance. She tried as best she could to keep up with the regular household responsibilities. Their children helped when they could, but they had work schedules and families of their own to care for. She stopped going to church. At first, church members called, made quick visits, and left a variety of gifts. After a while, this activity dwindled to an occasional call or visit. Mrs. P lost weight and became extremely fatigued. She believed her strong faith in God was keeping her going, but sometimes she felt like she couldn't continue.

Two years later, Mr. P had his other leg removed. Because of Mrs. P's precarious health, their children strongly suggested nursing home care, as recommended by the doctors. Mr. P felt betrayed because he had expressed the desire never to enter a nursing home and felt that his wishes should be honored. Mrs. P agreed that it was probably the best thing to do, but she felt a deep sense of guilt. Her guilt was intensified by members of the church who chided her that "African Americans shouldn't do that" (Carter, 1988).

Caring for an elder in the home of an adult child also brings demands and changes that are difficult for the elder and the caregiving family. Difficulties for the elder are often connected to the loss of revered surroundings and friend relationships, change from independent living to dependence on the caregiving family, and fears of being a burden. Difficulties for the caregiving family are often connected to an overload of responsibilities, conflict between caregiving and job and family responsibilities, and curtailment of prior activities in and outside the home. Both the elder and the caregiving family may worry about finances. And both may experience a sense of intrusion when professional caregivers are needed to provide support services.

The difficulties both the elder and the caregiving family experience can cause conflict, anger, and confusion. And unless they have opportunities to work through the difficulties and their impact on everyone involved, persons are prone to develop a sense of isolation and of "being trapped."

The family of Mr. and Mrs. H was headed in the direction of feeling trapped at the end of their first year of caregiving for Mrs. H's mother. The mother, aged seventy-eight, had been a widow for several years, and over that time, she was diagnosed with Alzheimer's disease. She was aware of her move from the familiar surroundings of her home, and she had frequent bursts of anger at what she called "being kidnapped." She also had periods where she cried uncontrollably. She had to be watched constantly because of her wandering, and she needed help with eating, bathing, dressing, and toilet use.

In trying to balance caregiving with work schedules and child rearing, the husband and wife caregivers found themselves with less and less couple time and individual private time. At year's end, family conflict was great, and they found themselves longing for an alternative yet feeling guilty about their longing. However, they moved toward some resolution when they joined a support group for adult caregivers and discovered that others were struggling with similar problems and feelings. They also hired part-time service providers that allowed them some free time.

Give Support Through Visits and Set Up Support Groups

Caregivers receive a great sense of support and relief when others visit them. When there are no contacts, or if they receive critical comments from others, they develop a sense of isolation that is health-threatening for them (Bumagin and Hirn, 1990). Visits may also take the form of practical help and respite events. Practical help might include doing household tasks for the caregiver to which the caregiver gives consent. Respite events take place when the church provides a friendly sitter for the sick elder while another friend invites the caregiver to a social event agreed on by the caregiver.

Even severely ill elders also need human contact. To deny it repudiates their humanness by treating them as though they were already dead. They also need to share, if possible, their feelings about their situation and to talk honestly about their life and death. They need to be assured that they will not be forsaken, no matter what happens. And if in fact there is a sense that the dying elder needs permission to die, that elder needs a close caring other who will grant it (Bumagin and Hirn, 1990).

Another way the soul community can give support to families and caregivers of seriously and terminally ill elders is its establishment of support groups. These groups are intentional gatherings of family members and caregivers who commit to regular meetings for the purpose of being for one another a compassionate presence, listener, and discernment partner. The importance of these groups lies in the emotional nurture, encouragement, and information resulting from mutual caring. Such groups may be initiated and facilitated by either clergy or laypersons. The initiator or facilitator takes on responsibility for announcing the formation of a group, clearly stating its purpose, meeting times, and group guidelines. As facilitator, the clergy or layperson guides the group in building an environment of trust, affirmation, and open communication.

We have already learned about the nature and importance of the compassionate presence, listener, and discernment guide in the promotion of wellness. Each one is equally necessary in providing support in situations of elders' severe, debilitating, or terminal illness. However, they become effective to the extent that we have some prior awareness of the kinds of family situations on which we focused earlier.

Life and Death Decision Making

African American families, like others, struggle with life and death decisions, particularly in cases of an elder's terminal illness or irreversible coma. Families are typically asked to decide on a living will, if there is none. Signing the living will is basically a declaration that says, "If I have a terminal condition and there is no hope of recovery, I do not want my life prolonged by artificial means" (United Methodist Association, 1994b). Artificial means are medical procedures such as cardiopulmonary resuscitation (CPR), use of a respirator, and forced feeding.

Thinking about life's end is not easy. Family members, in particular, have a hard time when the decision about life support becomes theirs to make. But if the dying person has not expressed a preference verbally or in writing, family members cannot escape having to decide. Yet in interviews with elders, over and over again, they voiced sentiments like those of an eighty-four-year-old woman: "One thing that I do not want my family to do is to put me on life support systems. I do not want that kind of strain on my family or myself. I would not want to prolong my life in that way knowing that I only had a little time left. I haven't told my family that, though. I need to do that." A sixty-five-year-old woman said, "No, Lord! I would rather be out of my misery; and I certainly wouldn't want my family to have that worry on them. But no, I haven't talked with anyone in my family about this yet."

An eighty-seven-year-old woman said, "You know, if I were dying, I would want to go on and die. I would not like to be put on life support systems. Though I have talked with my family about my funeral arrangements, I have not expressed to them my wishes about life support systems, not yet anyway." And an eighty-six-year-old man said, "Now, for the question of whether or not I want to be put on life support systems, the answer is, 'No, ma'am, I do not! If I am not ever going to get well or be any more good, I wouldn't want to linger around.' No, I have not talked to my family members about this matter. I probably would, though, if I felt that I was coming to that point."

When families have to make life and death decisions, they do so on the basis of deeply held views about what they believe is ethically, morally, and religiously right. They also make decisions on how they answer the question "Can I let go?" (United Methodist Association, 1994a).

A case in which an elder and family members had to decide was that of Rev. S, a sixty-eight-year-old African American male who was diagnosed with terminal colon cancer. After three hospitalizations, two surgeries, and chemotherapy over a period of six months, he and his family were told that the disease had not been arrested and that it had in fact spread throughout the lymphatic system and to other organs.

The doctors gave the option for more chemotherapy for purposes of at least slowing the progression of the disease. At first, the family was stunned by the news. For a time, they seemed frozen in silence. But Rev. S broke the silence and made clear that he had given much thought and prayer to his situation and wished no further treatment and no extraordinary measures, including no forced feeding to prolong his life should he become comatose. He expressed his desire to die with dignity at home. He also said he was not afraid to die because he believed that Jesus Christ had prepared a place for him at the welcome table. The family of Rev. S affirmed his decision. He was cared for at home with hospice help until he died.

With ever-increasing awareness of euthanasia and suicide as choices elders make when confronted with debilitating or terminal illness, churches dare not evade a discussion about them. Even though we think the elders in our churches are not considering such alternatives, it is important to be aware of the agonizing situations they may be facing, and it is equally important to listen for any hint of an elder's interest in them and engage discussion about them. Likewise, it is important to pay close attention to the function of our community in their lives.

The communal context is a pivotal environment for a discussion of these issues. It is pivotal because through it we model the meaning of the African proverb cited several times so far, "I am because we are, and because we are, I am." The essence of this proverb is akin to Westley's statement that "we are bonded to one another, no matter how alone we might feel" (1995, p. 49).

Not only do we need to model this understanding, but we also need to explore the religious understanding of life as a gift and consider the impact on the community of choosing our own death. Likewise, we need to invite recognition that when the community fails persons, their aloneness begins. Our failure as a community has consequences for people's lives.

The remainder of this chapter proposes a process and guidelines for developing a community of compassion in life and death situations. A critical starting point for the process is breaking the silence surrounding dying and death so that issues requiring decisions can be looked at critically and made from an informed stance.

Breaking the Silence

Recall the statements of elders who were clear about their stance on life supports for themselves but had not communicated it to family members. Recall also that the family of Rev. S was "frozen in silence" when confronted with his impending death. Reverend S pierced the silence by expressing his desire to die with dignity, but the typical response to dying and death in our society is one of "heavy silence" (May, 1987, p. 175). Becoming a community of compassion and allowing for the authentic expression of reverence for life and respect for persons cannot happen in a context of silence. But how can the silence be broken?

The beginning of the process of breaking the silence may involve confronting feelings of the awesomeness of death itself. A part of this may entail questioning about what it means to "let go." It may mean, as well, exploring the pros and cons of life support measures. It may also mean that we discuss what we understand about God's presence in Christ and hope for ongoing life after death.

The essential matter in breaking the silence is not simply confronting the questions that are raised. It is being present for and listening to the real life and death dilemmas that people face. For example, it was only when Rev. S was listened to by the family members that the family together was able to act on the decision for no further treatment and to make the necessary plans for providing care that ensured respect and dignity in the dying process. Consequently, a community of compassion that seeks to break the silence must be a community that is able to be in solidarity with others. Only through solidarity are we truly able to listen and hear others.

Critical Reflection and Discernment

Breaking the silence opens the way to critical reflection and discernment. Critical reflection and discernment are best undertaken in the context of a community of compassion, which the soul community has to be. Within this context, we may consider whether medical technology assists God's efforts to continue life or whether technology is an interference in God's intent for the order of human life and death.

In the context of the compassionate community, we as Christians may also ask the questions of whether we believe God to be a "hangman God" or a God who initiates relationship with us, acts concretely in our lives, and continues in solidarity with us throughout our mortal life and in the hereafter. Moreover, in a caring atmosphere where sharing can safely take place, myriad questions can be addressed by families and elders in advance of critical illness and the need for making life and death decisions. Indeed, it is essential for churches to encourage individuals and families to plan for the difficult and unexpected times of life, to help family, caregivers, and others avoid some of the burdens and stress they may experience in making difficult choices during crises (Deets, 1992, p. 1). Likewise, a compassionate atmosphere allows families dealing with critically ill elders and immediate life and death decisions to raise myriad questions. People can feel free to ask, Are life supports really needed? How long can life be sustained by these supports, and what do we need to know about the quality of life given a particular situation? Is it feasible to undergo numerous surgeries and treatments if there are questionable results, and what difference might ongoing treatments make? Would I want my parent or myself to endure pain and suffering? Will I be able to handle the expenses, and how do I feel about it if I can't? Will my family's needs be met if financial resources are used for medical expenses? How will I feel if I have to make the decision for a living will for my parent or spouse? How do I feel about making the decision for myself now?

The fact that people have a compassionate and supportive community in which to reflect critically and discern what to do does not mean necessarily that their decisions are influenced by that community. What it does mean is that the community is there for them and participates with them in the discernment process. In this way, honor is experienced not simply by elders but also by their families and the whole community.

Practical Guidelines

The following practical guidelines build on approaches of proven value in preparing for the end of elders' lives (Rando, 1986, pp. 29–34; LaGreca, 1986, p. 87).

1. Attempt to break any silence that precludes discussion of dying and death and to articulate a vision for how the soul

community can form a context of compassionate, trusting, warm love, where persons enter into solidarity with those who seek answers to questions, who must make decisions, and who suffer.

2. Listen to elders and family members, attend to their concerns and their grief, and be with them in their struggle with difficult questions.

3. Create educational ministries that assist persons' understanding of life as a gift from God for which individuals and the whole community are stewards.

4. Witness through the ritual and relational life of the church the Christian hope exemplified in the life, death, and resurrection of Jesus Christ and the dignity of human life amid complex issues and tragic situations.

5. Consider the psychosocial, spiritual, and economic needs of elders and their families as part of the soul community's concern for multidimensional well-being. Advocate for and provide these resources when needed.

6. Accept as a gift the ways in which critically ill and dying elders minister to the well, and respect the desires they may have for reciprocal caring.

7. Affirm the use of technology as a gift of our age as well as the right of elders and family members to make informed decisions regarding its use.

8. Help survivors in their grieving in advance of an elder's death, facilitate grieving after the fact, and plan for practical and social considerations that need to be addressed.

Concluding Commentary

In this chapter, we have explored key ways of ministering to elders and their families given the realities of health problems among African Americans. We have also considered approaches to ministry in situations of elders' illness and with regard to life and death decisions. We learned that health promotion is an essential aspect of the soul community's goal of improving the well-being of elders. We also learned of the necessity of community responses of support and compassion in times of illness and in elders' and their families' processes of making life and death decisions.

Questions for Reflection

1. How aware have you been of the health risks that African Americans face? What measures have you, your family, and your church taken to minimize these risks?

2. In what ways does your church minister to elders who are ill or experiencing physical mobility difficulties?

3. With what stories in this chapter did you identify? How did you feel as you were reading them? What suggestions did you get for acting in similar situations about which you are aware?

4. What actions does your church need to take in matters of the health, illness, and death of its members? What might your role be in promoting these actions?

11

HONORING AND SHARING OUR ELDERS' WISDOM

Edith Dalton Thomas, Anne Streaty Wimberly, Edward P. Wimberly

I AM PROUD TO CALL MYSELF an African American elder. I am sixty-nine years old and anticipate my rite of passage to retirement in another year. My African ties are strong. One son was born in Zaïre, and another is named Ghana. An African belief is "Kind words can never die, nor will they ever die." I believe these words because of what I remember of my ancestors. These words are repeated in a song. I myself want to pass along kind words to those who follow me.

At a family reunion, my family adopted a ritual growing out of African wisdom. It established twelve seats on a council of elders. When a seat is vacated by death, it is filled by the oldest of the children of that elder's generation. We recognized that there is something of value that passes on from elder to younger members that give lineage and continuity—a treasure from the lineage that passes on through the children as representatives of the elder.

o

This brief story was shared by an African American man who had strong family ties and cultural links to Africa. His understanding of the world includes a perspective of the place of elders in the overall scheme of life, something that has been lost in the youth-oriented culture in the United States. He recognizes that honoring elders is not just for the sake of the elders but also for the healthy survival of the community and for the generations that come after the elders.

This chapter attends to the importance of elders' resourceful participation in the church as a soul community. In it, we will examine this participation from the standpoint of the stewardship role of the elder. Our premise is that without this role, the soul community cannot survive. This role also casts elders as repositories of wisdom in community life. Stewardship is understood as guardianship over the values and stories of the soul community, and this responsibility is properly assigned to the church member with the most maturity in years and the most lived experience. Stewardship is rooted in an awareness that the treasures of the soul community must be passed on to the next generation and that these treasures—the values and traditions—can be passed on only if elders are regular participants in the life of the soul community.

On this basis, we will explore the role of elders as storytellers, Bible interpreters, and guides in practical wisdom in the ritual life of the church as a soul community. We will also be guided by the understanding that this role is an essential one in any arena where people gather to celebrate their religious and communal values through rites and ceremonies. Of critical importance in the ritual and ceremonial life of the church is the role of the elder as bard or poet whose role is to tell the story of the life of the community in creative ways in ceremonial settings.

A key realization underlies what we will consider here. We live in a culture that emphasizes technological and skilled knowledge over the wisdom of tradition and historical understandings. Many people in American culture think that we can get along without the wisdom of tradition and understanding that comes from experience. This is true if we think of life solely in market, consumer, product, money, and efficiency terms. However, when we think of life lived in community, in relationships, and in conflict, the wisdom of the past and of the elders is indispensable.

We seek answers to the major value-oriented and spiritually provocative problems confronting our society and evidenced in the marketplace. Is there not something of the wisdom of the elders that can help us? There is a permanent place for elders in our society and in the soul community. Without them, the well-being of the community and its quality of life are impaired. The inclusion of elders in the soul community is an absolute necessity for the survival of all.

Indeed, elders demonstrate their solidarity with all others in community when they share themselves.

Including the Elders in the Soul Community

The elders are essential to the vitality of the soul community. This reality is contained in the following testimony of a young adult African American man, who spoke during a retreat where congregation leaders met to do long-range planning. The retreat began with a time of storytelling: members of the church told what they knew about the church's founding, establishment, development, and ongoing life.

> What I remember about church as a youngster was the positive support that I received from the older members of the church. It was different than it is now. In the past, the older members really cared about you. They seemed to be interested in us and desired the best for us. When we came to the church for Sunday school, choir rehearsal, or Sunday morning worship, the elders made us feel welcomed. We felt we belonged. They even made a fuss over us by telling us that we were the future and had to be trained for our roles in the future church. They trained us as well. They taught us how to behave, how to pray, how to usher, and other things. They allowed us to have a youth day where we got to lead. We looked forward to being in church because it was motivational. I am still involved in the church today because of the positive way I was received by the elders when I was growing up.
>
> Unfortunately, that kind of positive atmosphere is gone today. There seems to be more resentment toward the youth. We had youth choirs and were welcomed to sing at least once a Sunday. I wish that the youth of today could really experience what I experienced. I wonder if it would be possible to recapture what we once had so that our youth could return to the church.

This young man articulated the significance of elders in his life growing up in the church. He also felt that this element is missing from the church today. The elders who were at the planning retreat were excited that this young man saw a role for them in the life of the church. Many of the elders themselves did not believe that they had a role to play and sensed that they were of no significance at all to the younger generation. When the elders heard that there were at least some young adults who felt that they had an indispensable role to play, they began the planning process for their roles as encouragers and supporters of the spiritual growth and development of children and youth. They began to reenvision their role as stewards of the wisdom of the past and bards of the stories of the faith, newly aware of their importance. These elders had to be told by young people that their role was significant before they themselves believed they had a role to play.

The Place of Storytelling

The role of elders in the life of the church as a soul community must be enacted through sharing their stories with the several generations comprising that community. We must create places and events in the life of the church where elders can tell their own stories. Part of church renewal is hearing and remembering the stories and envisioning the church's direction based on them.

What elders say when they tell their stories can help us envisage their significance for maintaining a sense of community. The stories they share help build community and strengthen communal bonds. By eliciting and listening to their stories, we affirm the value of soul in our community life. Here is an example of the kinds of stories elders tell:

> I am one hundred and one years old. I was born in Fayette County, Georgia, and grew up in that section of the country. Later I went to New York to serve as a Pullman porter. It was a handy way to work my way through college. The sleeping car was a serviceable operation before the airplane came into being. I have two sons. One was named for me, and I can call him and he comes in a hurry. I don't know what else to say about me. There are some things credible and some maybe not credible. But I have never been arrested or served time for any criminal behavior. Pray for me not necessarily that I will live another hundred years, but if God wants me to, it is all right.

Another elder says:

> I am eighty years old. My parents helped get five children through life. My father led morning prayer every morning and

gave the table blessing at each meal with all in the family present. Mother taught good behavior at all times and by eye contact from the choir where she sang. She could correct whatever
we might have been doing. I was the oldest of the three girls and
remember my mother's words before she died—"walk upright,
straight like a million dollars even though you may not have a
dime." On mother's deathbed, she expressed pride in her girls'
not having given her any trouble. The message I received is this:
if you live right and put your hand in God's hand, he will lead
you where you want to go.

These words come from people who know what it means to be
part of an extended family and deeply grounded in a faith community. One of the sad things about our society today is that communal
meals, time in church as family, and family reunions do not happen
enough. But our hope lies in our recognizing that these routine family rituals are essential for our survival as individuals and as a group.
They are indispensable to our future as African Americans. From
our elders we can get the message that these relationships are extremely important to maintain.

The following is a ritual that was used at a family reunion. The
host speaks:

> All who believe in God's mercy and grace will meet their loved
> ones face to face, where time is endless and joys are unbroken
> and only the words of love are spoken.
>
> As we gather this evening in celebration of our fifty-fifth fam-
> ily reunion, we must never forget our forebears. For it is in them
> that the unbroken circle of love has brought us to this day.
>
> So we call upon our elder to light a candle in honor of our
> forebears. [*The eldest family member lights a gold candle.*] And
> we call upon our elder to light a candle in honor of life. [*The el-
> dest family member lights a white candle.*]

Two young people then come to the elder to receive each of the
lighted candles. Each then takes the lighted candle to his or her seat
and uses it to light the candle of the person in the next seat until
everyone's candle has been lit.

Following this, the host leads the family in a litany involving the
letters of the family name, Nelson.

Call to our forebears.

N is for *never.* May we never forget our journey in honor of
our forebears.

E is for *excellence* in all that we do.

L is for *life* and *love,* which our forebears have handed
down to us and which sustain us.

S is for the renewing of our *spirits* in honor of our forebears.

O is for *others.* May we be mindful of each other in honor
of our forebears.

N is for *new beginnings.* May we seek greater wisdom in
honor of our forebears.

This litany is followed by a prayer of remembrance for family members who are no longer alive.

Churches don't have to wait for special times for elders to tell their stories so that they can contribute to community life. The regular ritual life of the church can have moments of recollection where the past is rehearsed as a way to celebrate key values that the faith community wants to keep alive.

Elders and Narrative

Also pivotal to understanding the inclusion of elders in the soul community is the role of storytellers in the African and African American tradition. In Chapter Two, we were reminded of our tradition of storytelling handed down to us from the *griots* in Africa. The *griots* were the elders. This tradition is pointed to in many publications, and it is prevalent in preaching, pastoral care, and Christian education (Mitchell and Lewter, 1986; E. P. Wimberly, 1991; Wimberly, 1994b; Wimberly and Wimberly, 1986).

When African Americans needed an orientation to make sense out of the racial nonsense they encountered in the United States, they turned to the stories the elders told about faith. The faith stories came mainly from the Holy Scripture; and in Scripture, they found reason for living, perspective for viewing their oppression, and hope for overcoming racism. The stories that the elders told provided a rich repository of characters, roles, and story plots with which African Americans could identify.

This tradition is so strong among adults over thirty in the African American community that most of them know all the key personalities of the Bible—even adults who do not frequent the church. African American homeless men and women are very well acquainted with these stories and draw on them to explicate their predicament (Wimberly, 1987). Through the stories that elders tell in church, in the home, at family reunions, and in other informal face-to-face settings, the values of the past are communicated from generation to generation.

Hospitality and Stewardship

The testimony of the young man at the church planning retreat earlier in this chapter showed us that African American elders placed hospitality at the center of church life. What attracted the children and youth to the church was the welcome they received from the elders. To be hospitable means to show community solidarity in welcoming ways, ways that embrace and invite rather than exclude and alienate.

The biblical notion of hospitality has influenced African Americans' understanding of the soul community. This value undergirds the soul community's understanding of itself as an extended family. Hospitality refers to how we welcome and receive strangers (Wimberly and Wimberly, 1991). The New Testament communicates that hospitality is extended to kin not based on blood lines. This was essential in the early Christian church, where often the only factor that congregants had in common was their belief in Jesus Christ, and it was an expression of the Christianity they espoused.

During slavery, African Americans found it difficult to keep track of blood kinship lines because slave families were usually separated on the auction block. But this did not prevent African Americans from relating to one another as family. They appropriated the African tribal extended family values based on fictive kin or nonblood relationships. Thus the early slaves saw themselves as kin in much the same way as people in the early church saw themselves as kin.

This tradition of viewing others as kin regardless of blood ties has influenced the formal and informal adoption practices of African Americans even today. According to Andrew Billingsley in *Climbing Jacob's Ladder* (1992), formal and informal adoption is practiced by African Americans disproportionately more than by Euro-Americans. Welcoming into the family went far beyond blood lines. In this context, there are no strangers; all are in the family, from infants to elders. Biblical and cultural legacies influence this notion of kinship.

The young man at the retreat also referred to the importance of elders in training young people about their role in church life. He was highlighting the elders as transmitters to younger generations of the wisdom treasures of the past.

The biblical concept of the steward undergirded African American elders' understanding of their role in the church as a soul community. We have already learned in Chapter Four that biblical stewardship refers to guardianship of the mysteries of God, and these mysteries include the values and traditions that express these mysteries (*Interpreter's Dictionary,* 1990). All Christians were thought to be stewards (1 Cor. 4:1; Gal. 4:2; 1 Pet. 4:10). Those who were stewards were thought to be the most spiritually mature (Gal. 4:2).

In African tradition, elders were also the stewards of the community's values, and it was the elders' function to preserve these values and pass them on to the next generation. Armed with the biblical faith tradition and African tradition, African American elders have been given a significant stewardship role in the church. It is through them that the values of the faith tradition are passed on, and this is an indispensable role that elders as stewards play.

In summary, African American elders play an essential role in what we understand to be the soul community. This role includes assisting all African Americans to place who they are and what they do in historical perspective. For example, it is the elders who know the stories of the faith tradition and of the community. It is they who can recite this history, particularly in the ceremonial or ritualistic life of the faith community. Community members enter the process of interpreting and reinterpreting their lives in light of this history. They regard their lives as meaningful because they have a meaningful history.

Elders also help soul community members visualize the complexity of human behavior, and they enable people to have hope despite the bad things that happen in life. They help soul community members know the meaning of the cultural expressions "Trouble don't last always" and "Truth crushed to earth will rise again." Likewise, they help community members know the meaning of "You reap what you sow." Such wisdom enables soul community members to envisage a hopeful future because it is growing out of a meaningful past. And elders help younger community members see God at work in their lives, ensuring the future of the members of the soul community.

Fostering the Rediscovery of Elders' Roles in Church and Family

The young man who spoke at the planning retreat enabled the elders to rediscover their function in the life of the church. The elders began to reenvision their place in the faith community based on their rediscovering their role.

A panel of elders discussed their views on the role of elders in church and family. They clearly communicated that there are many ways the wisdom of elders can be passed on to succeeding generations. We can be teachers by example, mentors, and storytellers, they said. There was a sense that taking on these leadership roles is a way for them to pass on to others the roles that their elders had taken with them. One elder told of what her mother taught her:

> I am sixty-three years old and have three children, four grandchildren, and one great-grandchild. I have always been a homemaker and kept many other children with my own. Most of my life has been wrapped around children. I enjoy singing, and I have taught Sunday school. My mother was a little lady with strong ways and advice. In other words, you had to listen to her. She was a strong believer in God, prayed a lot, and taught her children to work, watch, and pray. Mother could be heard praying anytime, even in the garden. I learned a lot from her, and I've found that prayer works in any situation.

The panel of elders also highlighted the importance of families' researching their cultural, family, and church history and recording key events and figures. They stressed that doing this helps people discover their identity, form values, and connect with sustaining traditions. Akin to this is what younger people learn about their history through hearing what the elders say. Several persons in the panelists' audience expressed a sense of awe at "the history the elders had made" and "how inspiring their lives are." The historical testimony of a ninety-one-year-old panelist evoked numerous responses:

> I am ninety-one years old. I was named for my mother. I have had operations on each hip and sometimes have to walk with a cane. I was married sixty-four years before my husband died. At Tuskegee Institute, my husband and I worked with children and teenagers before coming to Gammon Seminary, where I worked

with students' wives. At age fifty-five, I retired from Spelman
College's Extension School for Children. I had earned a master's
degree in child psychology. I learned to love everybody without
regard to race.

The panelists also said that it is their role—in fact, the role of
everyone—to show affection to others and to contribute to a nurturing environment knowing that this provides hospitality and welcoming. They recognize that for many elders today, doing this is
inescapable because of responsibilities given them to raise grandchildren. And they emphasized the role that elders can play in stressing
the importance of education, discipline, high moral values including
respect for others and for oneself, and worthy goals in life. These
panelists and other elders recognize that it is not always easy for
them to take on this latter role in a society where the young rely so
much on peer groups. They recognize that young people do not always want to hear what they have to say. But they believe it is important to try. They see their role as conveying to others some of the
important lessons they themselves learned. And their stories are one
way they tell what they believe they should do as well as what they
hope for the next generation. One elder shared the following:

> I am seventy years old and have two children, three grandchil-
> dren, and two sisters. As a child, we were taught strong family
> ties and sharing. Our mother was a singing mother. Music has
> been a part of the upbringing of every child who touched her
> life. Music not only helps keep you going but gives you disci-
> pline, if you take part. All of us had lessons to play some instru-
> ment. Church was an important part of our background. Our
> parents told us what they expected, and we in turn were ex-
> pected to hear what they had to say. We had no problems in lis-
> tening in school. Learning was important to us.

Another said, "I have three children, four grandchildren, and one
great-grandchild. I was an enforcement officer for thirty years. I am
now sixty-five years old and have been a part-time attorney since
1969. My father instilled in me that if I care enough about a job to
take it, do it well; and if money is scarce, pay your rent first so that
you will have a roof over your head."

What came through so clearly from these elders was their need to
be stewards and to carry out the stewardship tradition for the well-
being of all soul community members.

A Continuum of Roles

The soul community is an ideal context for welcoming the wisdom of elders and their resourceful participation. This forum for accepting the gifts of elders has a foundation in history. But to be a welcoming context, the soul community must recognize the gifts they bring, affirm the gifts they are giving, and promote their use in new and creative ways. A study of ten African American churches in the Atlanta area provides insights into the pastors' recognition of a continuum of roles through which the gifts of elders were being used and which the churches welcomed (Wimberly, 1979):

- *Leader.* This role was identified in all of the churches. It included elders' participation in official capacities such as treasurer, class leader, secretary, property manager, president of senior citizens' groups, Sunday school superintendent, chair of finance and stewardship committees, and member of leadership committees such as administrative boards, ecumenical affairs, health and welfare, mothers' boards, deacons' boards, family life, and pastor-parish relations committees.

- *Stabilizer.* In at least one instance, an elder served as the essential life force undergirding the church.

- *Consultant or adviser.* In three churches, elders served as advisers to the pastor, Sunday school classes, and young adult groups.

- *Oral historian.* In one of the ten churches, an elder served as the church historian.

- *Grandparent or surrogate grandparent.* In three churches, grandparents functioned as guides, storytellers, and providers of children's sermons. They also became surrogate grandparents to children whose parents were absent from Sunday school or church.

- *Caregiver.* In all ten churches, elders were identified as giving service to other elders or younger members through missionary societies, the mothers' board, senior programs, or visitation programs.

- *Repository of wisdom.* In two of the ten churches, elders were singled out as persons from whom both general and spiritual wisdom was expected.

Helping Elders Move into Stewardship

The elder panelists to whom we referred earlier were clear about their needs to be stewards and about ways in which they and other elders might carry out that role. Pastors in the aforementioned study also recognized the gifts of stewardship that elders brought to their churches. But problems can arise in accommodating the elders' needs to be stewards. In fact, in five of the ten churches in the study, elders were characterized as controllers who dominated church responsibilities to varying degrees, sometimes at the expense of younger members (Wimberly, 1979). The antagonisms resulting from this perception of elders can create an environment of resistance.

We have already learned in Chapter Four about attitudinal, interactional, and contextual resistance and ways of confronting it. However, we must not overlook the important role the entire soul community must play in helping elders achieve Christian stewardship. The community must see its role as providing both the expectation that elders will serve as stewards and the structure in which to do so (Whitehead and Whitehead, 1979). How does the community engage this role?

The community becomes the facilitator of elder stewardship first by moving away from a generational, competitive attitudinal framework toward an intergenerational, interdependent one. This shift requires that we deal with our heads, hearts, and actions. It requires all of the following:

- We must recognize and affirm elders as having the capacity and the need to care for the Christian household and to hand on the faith.

- We must dispel the myth that aging, retirement, and inactivity are synonymous. The reality is that retired persons do not necessarily feel or act old. People who have cut back on work or retired completely or who are pursuing new vocations rarely seek also to reduce their participation in the soul community.

- We must understand that the distance older people have traveled in life can provide a panoramic view of Christian growth and development from which the various generations can learn.

- We must listen and respond in supportive ways to the suggestions of elders regarding how and when they wish to serve.

- We must reinforce interdependent communal values that define the soul community. This includes the recognition that the various generations need one another, that we are one body, that we are to strive to keep the unity of the God's spirit, and that we are to walk together in love in the same manner as Christ loved us.

The soul community must also provide concrete opportunities for elders to be stewards. In addition to ones identified in the study mentioned earlier, the following seven are pivotal:

- Create occasions for elders to share their stories.
- Celebrate deceased African American heroes.
- Encourage older members to share the history of African American churches and stories of growing up in the African American community and in the United States.
- Conduct intergenerational retreats that include storytelling and listening as well as communal worship, meals, and play.
- Have a senior recognition day to affirm the elders' gifts of stewardship.
- Provide opportunities for seniors to come together for mutual uplifting and shared storytelling.
- Have elders serve as ushers and greeters during worship.

Elders as Lifelong Learners

In addition to their participation in the soul community as stewards whose gifts contribute to the care and future of the community, African American elders seek to participate as learners. They want to deepen their faith through Christian educational activities. When asked why they participate in such activities, the dominant response was that they seek spiritual guidance. They said that Christian education helps them make sense of past and present life struggles and provides both spiritual and social resources. As one elder said, "We have to put ourselves in a position to continue to learn and be spiritually uplifted. Life has its ups and downs. It is important to be reminded of what God's presence means. It's important to find out what can help carry us through life. For me, that's the only way I can make it, especially in the 'downs' of life."

For many African American elders, participation in Christian education has been a long-standing activity of great value. But in their later
years, it begins to serve important additional purposes. Elders report
that it revitalizes and uplifts them by giving them spiritual resources,
keeping them mentally and physically active, and maintaining social
ties and fellowship. Many find it helpful to study Scripture in tandem
with story sharing, prayer, and exploring health and family issues. For
others, simply the study of Scripture in Bible study groups is enough.

They also insist that there should be different places for different
educational opportunities: church, senior center, senior high-rise,
home, and nursing home. The home context is a particularly helpful
setting. One elderly woman said, "I find my women's study group,
which meets once a month, very rewarding. We meet at nine-thirty
in the morning, have coffee and cake or something good. We have a
devotional and a lesson and enjoy good fellowship. There are about
twenty in our group. Each meeting is in a different home, which
adds to the interest and seems more intimate."

In a study of fifty-five African Americans aged sixty-five and over
designed to discover what they want in Christian education, elders
identified five categories of activities (Wimberly, 1994a):

• *Faith introspection:* activities focused on prayer, meditation,
and life review. Elders want opportunities to deepen their spiritual
lives by engaging in and learning new approaches to these activities.
They see these activities as assisting them in making sense out of
past and present experiences and in their preparation for life's end.

• *Faith understanding:* activities such as Bible study and the
study of church doctrines and beliefs and church history. Elders see
these activities as enhancing their knowledge and understanding of
the Christian faith and themselves as guardians of the faith.

• *Faith sustenance:* activities that address retirement concerns
and options; material, physical, and mental well-being; gender-
related issues including health problems and widowhood; and issues
of grief, loss, and loneliness. Elders say that their faith is often tested
by their insufficient knowledge of how to address certain issues that
arise. They contend that Christian education ought to provide information and resource ideas to assist them in dealing with life issues.

• *Faith interaction:* activities focused on issues of interpersonal
relationships in family, church, and community. Elders indicate that
relationships often pose challenges to them, particularly with young
people. They are challenged by communication gaps and conflict be-

tween them and the young and by perceived lack of respect. They do not always know what to do about relational conflict. They believe that Christian educational activities should include talk about relational issues and information helpful in addressing these issues.

• *Faith service:* activities highlighting service in church, family, and community. Elders believe that living the Christian faith entails serving church, family, and community in whatever ways they can, however great or small, as long as one is able. But they do not always know where or how to serve. In addition, some elders discredit their wisdom and their talents, and some even discredit their value in the sight of God. For these reasons, elders said that Christian education should give them guidance on what it means to exercise faith through service in their elder adult years and how and where to do it.

The five categories the elders identified as foci for Christian education in which they participate are important matters for the soul community to take seriously. This is because they reflect the elders' concerns for every area of their well-being—spiritual, physical, psychological, social, and economic.

Concluding Commentary

The intent of this chapter was to provide key information about elders' participation as stewards in the life of the soul community. The chapter explored a foundation for the inclusion of elders as a significant part of the soul community. They were described as essential because their role functions are vital to the fulfillment of the goals of the community. We learned that the task of the soul community is to ensure elders' roles as resourceful participants in the community and as repositories of wisdom.

Questions for Reflection

1. In what ways are elders active participants in your church?
2. When and where do elders tell their stories?
3. How may your church assist elders in being stewards of the faith?
4. In what ways is Christian education responsive to the needs of elders?
5. To what extent are elders consulted about ways they might participate in the life of the church and ways the church might respond to them?

REFERENCES

Achtemeier, P. J. *Harper's Bible Dictionary.* San Francisco: Harper San Francisco, 1985.

American Association of Retired Persons. *Healthy Aging: Making Health Promotion Work for Minority Elders.* Washington, D.C.: American Association of Retired Persons, 1991a.

American Association of Retired Persons. *Staying Well: Health Promotion Programs for Older Persons.* Washington, D.C.: American Association of Retired Persons, 1991b.

American Association of Retired Persons. *Heart to Heart: Older Women and Heart Disease.* Washington, D.C.: American Association of Retired Persons, 1993a.

American Association of Retired Persons. *The Clergy: Gatekeepers for the Future.* Washington, D.C.: American Association of Retired Persons, 1993b.

American Association of Retired Persons. *Pep Up Your Life: A Fitness Book for Mid-Life and Older Persons.* Washington, D.C.: American Association of Retired Persons, 1995.

American Association of Retired Persons. *Perspectives in Health Promotion and Aging.* Washington, D.C.: American Association of Retired Persons, 1996.

American Association of Retired Persons and the Administration on Aging. *A Profile of Older Americans, 1993.* Washington, D.C.: U.S. Department of Health and Human Services, 1993.

American Society on Aging. *Serving Elders of Color: Challenges to Providers and the Aging Network.* San Francisco: American Society on Aging, 1992.

Anderson, N. "Aging and Hypertension Among Blacks: A Multidimensional Perspective." In J. S. Jackson (ed.), *The Black American Elderly: Research on Physical and Psychosocial Health.* New York: Springer, 1988.

Apfel, N. H., and Seitz, V. "Four Models of Adolescent Mother-Grandmother Relationships in Black Inner City Families." *Family Relations,* 1991, *40,* 421–429.

Aschenbrenner, J. "Extended Families Among Black Americans." *Journal of Comparative Family Studies,* 1973, 4, 257–268.

Ashbrook, J. B. *Minding the Soul: Pastoral Counseling as Remembering.* Minneapolis: Augsburg Fortress, 1996.

Baker, F. M. "Dementing Illness and Black Americans." In J. S. Jackson (ed.), *The Black American Elderly: Research on Physical and Psychosocial Health.* New York: Springer, 1988.

Bellah, R. N., and others. *Habits of the Heart: Individualism and Commitment in American Life.* Berkeley: University of California Press, 1985.

Berger, P. L. *Facing Up to Modernity: Excursions in Society, Politics, and Religion.* New York: Basic Books, 1977.

Biegel, D. E., and Farkas, K. "The Impact of Neighborhoods and Ethnicity on Black and While Vulnerable Elderly." In Z. Harel, P. Ehrlich, and R. Hubbard (eds.), *The Vulnerable Aged: People, Services, and Policies.* New York: Springer, 1990.

Billingsley, A. *Climbing Jacob's Ladder: The Enduring Legacy of African American Families.* New York: Simon & Schuster, 1992.

Bone, S. D. "Rural Minority Populations." *Generations,* 1991, 15(4), 63.

Bowen, M. *Family Therapy in Clinical Practice.* Northvale, N.J.: Aronson, 1978.

Boyd-Franklin, N. *Black Families in Therapy.* New York: Guilford Press, 1989.

Boykin-Barringer, L. "Health Status and Nutrition of the Minority Elderly: Implications for Geriatric Education." In M. S. Harper (ed.), *Minority Aging: Essential Curricula Content.* Washington, D.C.: U.S. Department of Health and Human Services, 1990.

Bradford, S. *Scenes in the Life of Harriet Tubman.* North Stratford, N.H.: Ayer, 1971.

Bumagin, V. E., and Hirn, K. F. *Helping the Aging Family.* New York: Springer, 1990.

Burt, S. E., and Roper, H. A. *Raising Small Church Esteem.* Bethesda, Md.: Alban Institute, 1992.

Burton, L., and Devries, C. "Challenges and Rewards: African American Grandparents as Surrogate Parents." *Generations,* 1992, 17, 51–54.

Buttrick, G. A. *The Interpreter's Bible.* Nashville, Tenn.: Abingdon Press, 1953.

Carter, J. H. "Health Attitudes/Promotions/Preventions: The Black Elderly." In J. S. Jackson (ed.), *The Black American Elderly: Research on Physical and Psychosocial Health,* 1988.

Carter, S. *Integrity.* New York: Basic Books, 1996.

Cedarleaf, J. L. "Listening Revisited." *Journal of Pastoral Care,* 1984, *38,* 310–316.

Cedarleaf, J. L. "Listening." In R. J. Hunter (ed.), *Dictionary of Pastoral Care and Counseling.* Nashville, Tenn.: Abingdon Press, 1990.

Chatters, L. M. "Subjective Well-Being Among Older Black Adults: Past Trends and Current Perspectives." In J. S. Jackson (ed.), *The Black American Elderly: Research on Physical and Psychosocial Health.* New York: Springer, 1988.

Chatters, L. M., and Taylor, R. J. "Life Problems and Coping Strategies of Older Black Adults." *Social Work,* 1989, *34*(4), 313–319.

Clements, W. M. "Science and Religion in Dialogue." In M. A. Kimble, S. H. McFadden, J. W. Ellor, and J. J. Seeber (eds.), *Aging, Spirituality, and Religion: A Handbook.* Minneapolis: Augsburg Fortress, 1995.

Copeland, N. E., Jr. *The Heroic Revolution: A New Agenda for Urban Youth Work.* Nashville, Tenn.: J. C. Winston, 1995.

Crum, M. *The Negro in the Methodist Church.* New York: Division of Education and Cultivation, Board of Missions and Church Extension, Methodist Church, 1951.

Curry, C. L. "Hypertension in the Black Elderly: Implications for Geriatric Education." In M. S. Harper (ed.), *Minority Aging: Essential Curricula Content for Selected Health and Allied Health Professions.* Washington, D.C.: U.S. Department of Health and Human Services, 1990.

Dancy, J., Jr. *The Black Elderly: A Guide for Practitioners.* Ann Arbor and Detroit: Institute of Gerontology, University of Michigan and Wayne State University, 1977.

Dass, R., and Gorman, P. *How Can I Help?* New York: Knopf, 1985.

Deets, H. B. *A Matter of Choice: Planning Ahead for Health Care Decisions.* (Rev. ed.) Washington, D.C.: American Association of Retired Persons, 1992.

Diallo, Y. D., and Hall, M. *The Healing Drum: African Wisdom Teachings.* Rochester, Vt.: Destiny Books, 1989.

Dilworth-Anderson, P. "Extended Kin Networks in Black Families." *Generations,* 1992, *19*(3), 29–32.

Dorfman, S. L. *Health Promotion for Older Minority Adults: A Review.* Washington, D.C.: American Association of Retired Persons and National Resource Center on Health Promotion and Aging, 1991.

Du Bois, W.E.B. *Efforts for Social Betterment Among Negro Americans.* Atlanta: Atlanta University Press, 1909.

Dudley, C. S. *Basic Steps Toward Community Ministry.* Washington, D.C.: Alban Institute, 1991.

Dyson, M. E. *Reflecting Black: African-American Cultural Criticism.* Minneapolis: University of Minnesota Press, 1993.

Ellor, J. W., and Bracki, M. A. "Assessment, Referral, and Networking." In M. A. Kimble, S. H. McFadden, J. W. Ellor, and J. J. Seeber (eds.), *Aging, Spirituality, and Religion: A Handbook.* Minneapolis: Augsburg Fortress, 1995.

Evans, J. H., Jr. *We Have Been Believers: An African-American Systematic Theology.* Minneapolis: Augsburg Fortress, 1992.

Flora, C. B., Flora, J. L., Spears, J. D., and Swanson, L. E. *Rural Communities.* Boulder, Colo.: Westview Press, 1992.

Foster, C. R. "The Pastor: Agent of Vision in the Education of a Community of Faith." In R. L. Browning (ed.), *The Pastor as Religious Educator.* Birmingham, Ala.: Religious Education Press, 1989.

Foster, C. R., and Shockley, G. S. *Working with Black Youth: Opportunities for Christian Ministry.* Nashville, Tenn.: Abingdon Press, 1990.

Fretheim, T. L. *Exodus: Interpretation—A Bible Commentary for Teaching and Preaching.* Louisville, Ky.: John Knox Press, 1991.

Genovese, E. D. *Roll, Jordan, Roll: The World the Slaves Made.* New York: Vintage Books, 1974.

Gilmore, J. *Too Young to Be Old.* Wheaton, Ill.: Harold Shaw, 1992.

Graham, W. R. "Pioneers and Prison Chaplaincy." In R. Hunter (ed.), *Dictionary of Pastoral Care and Counseling.* Nashville, Tenn.: Abingdon Press, 1990.

Hannerz, U. *Soulside: Inquires into Ghetto Culture and Community.* New York: Columbia University Press, 1969.

Harper, M. S. (ed.). *Minority Aging: Essential Curricula for Selected Health and Allied Health Professions.* Washington, D.C.: U.S. Department of Health and Human Services, 1990.

Harper, M. S., and Alexander, C. "Profile of the Black Elderly." In M. S. Harper (ed.), *Minority Aging: Essential Curricula Content for Selected Health and Allied Health Professions.* Washington, D.C.: U.S. Department of Health and Human Services, 1990.

Henderson, L. S., III, Kensinger, J. L., and RIVA Market Research. *Black Elders and Health-Related Issues: A Focus Group Study.* Washington, D.C.: American Association of Retired Persons, 1992.

Hilliard, A. G. *The Maroon Within Us: Selected Essays on African American Community Socialization*. Baltimore: Black Classic Press, 1995.

Howe, R. L. *The Miracle of Dialogue*. New York: Seabury Press, 1965.

Hultsch, D. F., and Deutsch, F. *Adult Development and Aging: A Life-Span Perspective*. New York: McGraw-Hill, 1981.

Hunter, R. *Dictionary of Pastoral Care and Counseling*. Nashville, Tenn.: Abingdon Press, 1990.

Interpreter's Dictionary of the Bible, Vol. 4. Nashville, Tenn.: Abingdon Press, 1990.

Jackson, J. S. "Negro Aged: Toward Needed Research in Social Gerontology." *Gerontologist*, 1971, *11*, 51–52;

Jackson, J. S. "Growing Old in Black America: Research on Aging Black Populations." In J. S. Jackson (ed.), *The Black American Elderly: Research on Physical and Psychosocial Health*. New York: Springer, 1988.

Johnson, H. M., Sr. "Pastoral Care Through a Lay Care Ministry." Doctoral dissertation, Interdenominational Theological Center, 1995.

Kaplan, S. *The Black Presence in the Era of the American Revolution, 1770–1880*. Washington, D.C.: Smithsonian Press, 1973.

Knierin, R. "Age and Aging in the Old Testament." In W. M. Clements (ed.), *Ministry with Aging: Designs, Challenges, Foundations*. San Francisco: Harper San Francisco, 1981.

Koff, T. H. "Aging in Place: Rural Issues." *Generations*, 1992, *16*, 53–55.

LaGreca, D. M. "Anticipatory Grief from the Clergy Perspective: Presuppositions, Experience, and a Suggested Agenda for Care." In T. A. Rando (ed.), *Loss and Anticipatory Grief*. Lexington, Mass.: Heath, 1986.

Levin, J. S., and Tobin, S. S. "Religion and Psychological Well- Being." In M. A. Kimble, S. H. McFadden, J. W. Ellor, and J. J. Seeber (eds.), *Aging, Spirituality, and Religion: A Handbook*. Minneapolis: Augsburg Fortress, 1995.

Lewis, H. "Blackways of Kent." In H. M. Nelsen, R. L. Yokley, and A. K. Nelsen (eds.), *The Black Church in America*. New York: Basic Books, 1971.

Lincoln, C. E., and Mamiya, L. H. *The Black Church in the African American Experience*. Durham, N.C.: Duke University Press, 1990.

Lockery, S. A. "Caregiving Among Rural and Ethnic Minority Elders." *Generations*, 1991, *15*(4), 59.

Manuel, R. C. "The Demography of Older Blacks in the United States." In J. S. Jackson, *The Black American Elderly: Research on Physical and Psychosocial Health*. New York: Springer, 1988.

Martin, J. M., and Martin, E. P. *The Helping Tradition in the Black Family and Community.* Silver Spring, Md.: National Association of Social Workers, 1985.

May, W. F. "The Sacral Power of Death in Contemporary Experience." In S. E. Lammers and A. Verhey (eds.), *On Moral Medicine.* Grand Rapids, Mich.: Eerdmans, 1987.

Mays, B. E., and Nicholson, J. W. *The Negro's Church.* New York: Arno Press, 1969.

Mbiti, J. *African Religions and Philosophy.* (Rev. ed.) New York: Doubleday, 1990.

McCulloch, B. J. "Aging and Kinship in Rural Context." In R. Blieszner and V. Hilkevitch (eds.), *Handbook of Aging and the Family.* Westport, Conn.: Greenwood Press, 1995.

McGadney, B. F., Goldver-Glen, R., and Pinkston, E. M. "Clinical Issues for Assessment and Intervention with the Black Elderly." In L. L. Carstensen and B. A. Edelstein (eds.), *Handbook of Clinical Gerontology.* New York: Pergamon Press, 1987.

Mead, M. *Culture and Commitment: A Study of the Generation Gap.* New York: Doubleday, 1970.

Mellon, J. (ed.). *Bullwhip Days: The Slaves Remember.* New York: Avon, 1988.

Mishkin, B. *A Matter of Choice: Planning Ahead for Health Care Decisions.* (Rev. ed.) Washington, D.C.: American Association of Retired Persons, 1992.

Mitchell, H., and Lewter, N. C. *Soul Theology.* San Francisco: Harper San Francisco, 1986.

Moberg, D. O. "Spiritual Maturity and Wholeness in the Later Years." In J. Seeber (ed.), *Spiritual Maturity in the Later Years.* Binghamton, N.Y.: Haworth Press, 1990.

Mockenhaupt, R. "Introduction: Self-Care for Older Adults: Taking Care and Taking Charge." *Generations,* 1993, *12,* 5–6.

Moore, T. *Soul Mates: Honoring the Mysteries of Love and Relationships.* New York: HarperCollins, 1994.

Muchow, J. A. "Self-Care as a Rural Healthcare Strategy." *Generations,* 1993, *17,* 29–32.

Mulholland, M. R. *Shaped by the Word: The Power of Scripture in Spiritual Formation.* Nashville, Tenn.: Upper Room, 1985.

Myers, W. R. *Black and White Styles of Youth Ministry: Two Congregations in America.* New York: Pilgrim Press, 1991.

National Council of Negro Women and National Eldercare Institute on Older Women. *The Income Status of Older Women: A Briefing Paper for the National Eldercare Institute on Older Women.* Washington, D.C.: National Council of Negro Women and National Eldercare Institute on Older Women, 1992.

Nichols, M. P., and Schwartz, R. C. *Family Therapy: Concepts and Methods.* Needham Heights, Mass.: Allyn & Bacon, 1991.

Oden, T. C. *Two Worlds: Notes on the Death of Modernity in America and Russia.* Downers Grove, Ill.: InterVarsity Press, 1992.

Paris, P. *The Spirituality of African Peoples: The Search for a Common Moral Discourse.* Minneapolis: Augsburg Fortress, 1995.

Pasteur, A. B., and Toldson, I. L. *Roots of Soul: The Psychology of Black Expressiveness.* New York: Anchor Books, 1982.

Patterson, S. C. *Ministry with Black Single Adults.* Nashville, Tenn.: Discipleship Resources, 1991.

Pedersen, J. *Israel: Its Life and Culture,* Vols. 3–5. London: Oxford University Press, 1964. (Originally published 1940.)

Pruchno, R. A., and Johnson, K. W. "Research on Grandparenting: Review of Current Studies and Future Needs." *Generations,* 1996, 20(1), 65–70.

Qualls, S. H. "Clinical Interventions with Later-Life Families." In R. Blieszner and V. Hilkevitch (eds.), *Handbook of Aging and the Family.* Westport, Conn.: Greenwood Press, 1995.

Rakowski, W. "Health Beliefs." In G. L. Maddox (ed.), *The Encyclopedia of Aging.* New York: Springer, 1987.

Rando, T. A. "A Comprehensive Analysis of Anticipatory Grief: Perspectives, Processes, and Problems." In T. A. Rando (ed.), *Loss and Anticipatory Grief.* Lexington, Mass.: Heath, 1986.

Schmall, V. L., and Pratt, C. C. "Family Caregiving and Aging: Strategies for Support." In G. A. Hughston, V. A. Christopherson, and M. J. Bonjean (eds.), *Aging and Family Therapy.* Binghamtom, N.Y.: Haworth Press, 1989.

Seeber, J. J. "Congregational Models." In M. A. Kimble, S. H. McFadden, J. W. Ellor, and J. J. Seeber (eds.), *Aging, Spirituality, and Religion: A Handbook.* Minneapolis: Augsburg Fortress, 1995.

Silverstone, B. M., and Horowitz, A. "Aging in Place: The Role of Families." *Generations,* 1992, 16(2), 27–30.

Skinner, J. H. "Aging in Place: The Experience of African American and Other Minority Elders." *Generations,* 1992, 16, 49–50.

Smith, M. S. "The Implications of Demographic Changes in the African American Aged Population for Formal and Informal Care Systems in the Twenty-First Century." In D. J. Jones (ed.), *Prescriptions and Policies: The Social Well-Being of African Americans in the 1990s.* New Brunswick, N.J.: Transaction, 1991.

Staples, R., and Johnson, L. B. *Black Families at the Crossroads: Challenges and Prospects.* San Francisco: Jossey-Bass, 1993.

Stewart, C. F. *African American Church Growth: Twelve Principles of Prophetic Ministry.* Nashville, Tenn.: Abingdon Press, 1994.

Tatenhove, F. V. "Evangelical Perspectives." In M. A. Kimble, S. H. McFadden, J. W. Ellor, and J. J. Seeber (eds.), *Aging, Spirituality, and Religion: A Handbook.* Minneapolis: Augsburg Fortress, 1995.

Taylor, R. J. "The Extended Family as a Source of Support to Elderly Blacks." *Gerontologist,* 1985, *25,* 488–489.

Taylor, R. J. "Religious Participation Among Elderly Blacks." *Gerontologist,* 1986, *26,* 630–636.

Taylor, R. J. "Aging and Supportive Relationships Among Black Americans." In J. S. Jackson (ed.), *The Black American Elderly: Research on Physical and Psychosocial Health.* New York: Springer, 1988.

Taylor, R. J., and Chatters, L. M. "Church-Based Informal Support Networks of Elderly Blacks." *Gerontologist,* 1986, *26,* 637–642.

Taylor, R. J., and Chatters, L. M. "Family, Friends, and Church Support Networks." In R. L. Jones (ed.), *Black Adult Development and Aging.* Berkeley, Calif.: Cobb & Henry, 1989.

Thurman, H. *Disciplines of the Spirit.* Richmond, Ind.: Friends United Press, 1987.

United Methodist Association of Health and Welfare Ministries. *Deciding About Life's End.* Dayton, Ohio: General Board of Global Ministries, 1994a.

United Methodist Association of Health and Welfare Ministries. *A United Methodist Resource Book About Advance Directives.* Dayton, Ohio: General Board of Global Ministries, 1994b.

Watson, W. H. "Family Care, Economics, and Health." In Z. Harel, E. A. McKinney, and M. Williams (eds.), *Black Aged: Understanding Diversity and Service Needs.* Thousand Oaks, Calif.: Sage, 1990.

Watson, W. H. "Ethnicity, Crime, and Aging." *Generations,* 1991, *15*(4), 53.

Westley, D. *When It's Right to Die: Conflicting Voices, Difficult Choices.* Mystic, Conn.: Twenty-Third Publications, 1995.

Whitehead, E. E., and Whitehead, J. D. *Christian Life Patterns: The Psychological Challenges and Religious Invitations of Adult Life.* New York: Doubleday, 1979.

Wiley, C. Y. "A Ministry of Empowerment: A Holistic Model for Pastoral Counseling in the African American Community." *Journal of Pastoral Care,* 1991, *45,* 355–364.

Wimberly, A. S. "Configurational Patterns in the Function of the Church for Aging Persons: A Black Perspective." *Journal of the Interdenominational Theological Center,* 1979, 6(2), 94–105.

Wimberly, A. S. "A Conceptual Model for Older Adult Curriculum Planning Processes Based on Normalization and Liberation." Doctoral dissertation, Georgia State University, 1981.

Wimberly, A. S. *Anecdotal Records.* Evanston, Ill.: Evanston Ecumenical Action Council, 1987.

Wimberly, A. S. "Across Cultural Boundaries: On Religious Education and Meanings." *Aging Today,* June-July 1991, p. 18.

Wimberly, A. S. "Christian Education for Health and Wholeness: Responses to Older Adults in Ethnic/Racial Contexts." *Religious Education,* 1994a, 89, 248–264.

Wimberly, A. S. *Soul Stories: African American Christian Education.* Nashville, Tenn.: Abingdon Press, 1994b.

Wimberly, A. S., and Wimberly, E. P. *The Language of Hospitality: Intercultural Relations in the Household of God.* Nashville, Tenn.: Cokesbury Press, 1991.

Wimberly, A. S., and Wimberly, E. P. "Pastoral Care of African Americans." In M. A. Kimble, S. H. McFadden, J. W. Ellor, and J. J. Seeber (eds.), *Aging, Spirituality, and Religion: A Handbook.* Minneapolis: Augsburg Fortress, 1995.

Wimberly, E. P. "A Conceptual Model for Pastoral Care in the Black Church Utilizing Systems and Crisis Theories." Doctoral dissertation, Boston University, 1976.

Wimberly, E. P. *Pastoral Counseling and Spiritual Values: A Black Point of View.* Nashville, Tenn.: Abingdon Press, 1982.

Wimberly, E. P. *African American Pastoral Care.* Nashville, Tenn.: Abingdon Press, 1991.

Wimberly, E. P., and Wimberly, A. S. *Liberation and Human Wholeness: The Conversion Tradition of Slaves and Ex-Slaves.* Nashville, Tenn.: Abingdon Press, 1986.

Woodson, C. G. *The History of the Negro Church.* Washington, D.C.: Associated Publishers, 1945.

INDEX

A

Abuse. *See* Elder abuse; Parental abuse

Accessibility, 69–70; exemplary churches of, 120–121; and health promotion, 157–158; parachurch examples of, 121; and pastoral care, 140; reflection questions for, 123–124; and rural transportation issues, 111. *See also* Metropolitan settings; Rural settings

Achtemeier, P. J., 38

Acts, 32

Administration on Aging, 14, 16

Adolescent rites of passage, 24, 29, 31

Adoption, 177–178

Adult church school, 7, 183–185

Advocacy, 133, 159

African American Church Growth (Stewart), 62–63

African American Clergy and Spouse Retirement Transition Project, 157

African American Pastoral Care (Wimberly), 142

African Methodist Episcopal (A.M.E.) Church, 7

African traditions: honoring elders in, 6–7, 8, 9–10, 19–20, 171–172; orientation to life in, 23–25; role of elders in, 28–30, 32, 176, 178

Age segregation, 20–21, 69

Aging: and African orientation to life, 23–25, 28; and Biblical orientation to life, 23, 25–28; and contemporary Western orientation to life, 23; fear of, and interactional resistance, 68–69; stereotypes about, 145

Aging-family stage, 84–85

Aging Network, 56

AIDS National Interfaith Network, 134

Alcohol, 151

Alcoholics Anonymous, 159

Alexander, C., 110, 113, 114

Allen African Methodist Episcopal Church, 120–121

Allen Home Care Agency, 120, 121

Allen Senior Citizens Community Center, 120

Alzheimer's Association, 133

Alzheimer's disease, 151, 163

American Association of Retired Persons (AARP), 14, 16, 56, 133, 151, 152, 154, 155, 156

American Red Cross, 113

American Society on Aging, 13–14, 151, 152

Ancestral orientation: African, 24–25; Hebrew, 26–28

Anderson, N., 152

Apfel, N. H., 79

Area Agency on Aging (AAA), 113, 130–131

Aschenbrenner, J., 9